Rechungpa:
A Biography of
Milarepa's Disciple

Based on:
The Mirror Illuminating
the Path to Liberation

je tshun ras chung rdo rje grags pa'i rnam thar rnam
mkhyen thar lam sal wai me long ye shes snag wa bzhugs so

A COMMENTARY BY

The Venerable Khenchen
Thrangu Rinpoche
Geshe Lharampa

TRANSLATED BY

Peter Roberts

EDITED BY

Sandy Garson

Namo Buddha Publications
P. O. Box 1083
Crestone, CO 81131
Phone: (719) 256-5367
Email: cjohnson@ix.netcom.com

Rinpoche's Web site: www.rinpoche.com
ISBN Number: 0-9628026-8-9

Acknowledgments

We would like to thank the many people who helped make this book
possible. First of all, we would like to thank Peter Roberts for translating this commentary, Gloria Jones for transcribing the tapes, and
Sandy Garson for being the editor. Sarah Harding translated the pref-
ace by His Holiness the 17th Karmapa, Urgyen Trinley Dorje.

We would like to thank Lama Wangchuk and his center
Kamtsang Sherab Choling of Honolulu, Hawaii, especially Kathleen
Bryan, Richard Melton, Linda Moore, Sandra Reibow, and Leilani
Sim-Godbehere for sponsoring and thus making this book possible.

The thangka of Rechungpa on the cover was done by Ngawang
Zangpo and the line drawings of the first lineage holders of
Rechungpa's Kagyu lineage were done by Jamyong Singhe.

Note

Technical terms are italicized the first time they are used to alert
the reader that they can be found in the Glossary.

The terms are given as they are pronounced. The actual spelling
of the Tibetan is given in the Glossary of Tibetan Terms.

*A portion of the proceeds of this book will go toward the support of the
Tibetan nuns at Karma Drubgyu Thargay Ling in Tilokpur, India. For more
information on supporting the nuns, contact: Kamtsang Sherab Choling,
P.O. Box 62261, Honolulu, HI, 96839. Telephone: (808) 735-2262.*

Table of Contents

His Holiness The Gyalwa Karmapa

༄༅། །བླ་མེད་རྒྱལ་བའི་བསྟན་པ་རིན་པོ་ཆེ་འཛམ་གླིང་ཐ་གྲུ་ཡོངས་ལ་ཁྱབ་བརྡལ་དུ་འགྲོ་བཞིན་པའི་སྐབས་འདིར། རིས་སུ་མ་མཆིས་པའི་སྟོན་པོན་མཁས་ཤིང་གྲུབ་པའི་སྐྱེས་ཆེན་དམ་པ་རྣམས་ཀྱི་མཛད་རྣམ་དང་། གསུང་མགུར་སོགས་བསྟན་པ་ལ་མཛད་པ་དཀར་པོའི་ཕྱག་རྗེས་ཀྱི་རིམ་པ་རྣམས་ཤེས་འདོད་ཡོད་པའི་དད་ལྡན་གྱི་མི་སྣ་ཉིན་རེ་བཞིན་འཕེལ་རྒྱས་སུ་འགྲོ་བ་རྣམས་ལ་ཆེད་གཉེར་དགོས་མཁོར་དམིགས་ཏེ། ཁྲ་འགྲུ་ན་མོ་བྱང་ཆུབ་ཞིང་འདུག་འཛིན་གྲུ་དང་། གོ་ཆོང་ཤེས་རབ་ཆོས་གླིང་གི་ཆོགས་པ་གཉིས་ནས་རྗེ་བཙུན་རས་ཆུང་རྡོ་རྗེ་གྲགས་པའི་མཛད་རྣམ་སྙིང་བསྡུས་ཤིག་དབྱིན་སྐད་དུ་ཕབ་བསྒྱུར་གྲུབ་ནས། པར་དུ་བསྐྲུན་པའི་ཕྱག་བསམ་དགེ་བའི་འདུག་པར་འབད་པ་བསྐྱེད་པ་ལ་ཡི་རང་གི་གནས་སུ་གྱུར། ལེགས་བྱས་འདི་ཉིད་ཀྱིས་གྲུབ་པའི་དབང་ཕྱུག་རས་ཆུང་རྡོ་རྗེ་གྲགས་པའི་སྐུ་གསུང་ཐུགས་ཀྱི་མཛད་པ་རྣམས་འགྲོ་བ་ཡོངས་ཀྱིས་ལེགས་པར་ཤེས་ཤིང་། བཀའ་ཆགས་བཟང་པོའི་འཕྲིན་པ་ལས་ཆེ་རབས་ཀུན་ཏུ་སྒྲུབ་བརྒྱུད་རིན་དོན་སྙིང་པོའི་བསྟན་པ་རིན་པོ་ཆེར་མི་ཕྱེད་པའི་དད་པ་ཐོབ་ཅིང་། དོན་གསལ་གདོང་པའི་གྲོལ་གཞིར་མཛད་དུ་ཕྱེད་པའི་སྨོན་ལམ་གྱི་མཚམས་སྦྱོར་བཅས། རྒྱགར་བྱང་ཕྱོགས་དག་རམས་ལ་གསང་ཆེན་རྒྱུད་སྙོད་དུ་མོ་ཆེའི་གཙུག་ལག་ལག་ཁང་ནས་ ༧དཔལ་ཀརྨ་པ་ ཨོ་རྒྱན་ཕྲིན་ལས་དབང་གི་རྡོ་རྗེས་ཕྱི་ལོ་ ༢༠༠༠ ཕྱི་ཟླ་ ༡༢ ཚེས་ ༡༠ ལ་བྲིས།

His Holiness The Gyalwa Karmapa

At this time, as the precious teachings of the incomparable Buddha spread throughout the whole world, the numbers of the faithful grow daily. These various people want to know of the great learned and accomplished holy beings that arose impartially in the past— the chronicles of their legacy of good activity for the doctrine, their deeds, their songs, and so forth.

With those needs and aspirations in mind, Namo Buddha Publications and Kamtsang Sherab Choling have collaborated to translate and publish this essential summary of the activities of Jetsun Rechung Dorje Drakpa. I rejoice in their efforts in this virtuous activity for which they have the highest altruistic intentions.

Through this well-conceived work, you will become thoroughly acquainted with the activities, sayings, and thoughts of this mighty adept, Rechung Dorje Drakpa. The positive impression it leaves may create a connection in your future lives with the precious teachings of the essential definitive meaning of the practice lineage, and you will gain undivided faith in them. May you then realize the clear light, the primordial ground of liberation.

With that prayer, the Glorious Karmapa, Urgyen Trinley Dorje, wrote this at Sangchen Gyuto Ramoche monastery in Dharmasala in Northern India on December 10, 2000.

Vajradhara (Tib. Dorje Chang)

Vajradhara pictured here is the dharmakaya form of the Buddha and is considered the origin of the Kagyu Lineage teachings.

Foreword

Milarepa was Tibet's greatest male saint and he had two major pupils—Gampopa and Rechungpa. Gampopa built monasteries and established the monastic tradition of the Kagyu lineage. Rechungpa took the dangerous journey to India three times and brought back many teachings which Marpa was not able to obtain. Not only this, but he was the recipient of many of Milarepa's oral teachings which no other student of his received.

Rechungpa's biography is unique in that it shows us what happens when a meditator has problems with following his teacher's advice. Rechungpa had two main obstacles to devotion: doubting the wisdom of his guru and having excessive pride. For example, when crossing a barren plain in Tibet, Milarepa asks Rechungpa to pick up a yak's horn. Rechungpa immediately misinterpreted this to mean that Milarepa was attached to some old relic. Actually Milarepa was going to use this horn to give Rechungpa a lesson on apparent and ultimate reality by placing himself inside the hollow horn during a hail storm. One may think that this is simply an exaggerated story of the pupil-teacher relationship, but a careful examination of the evidence will show that "miracles" such as rainbow body continue to occur even today without any scientific explanation as to how this is possible.

Besides not following the spiritual advice of his guru, Rechungpa also had a second obstacle to devotion which was his excessive pride. Pride results in believing that one has a high level of attainment, that one is actually equal or even more developed than one's guru. In the West where Hinduism and Buddhism are less than a hundred years old, it is not uncommon to find persons claiming that they or that their teachers are fully enlightened. This comes from a lack of understanding of what fully enlightened means. There are a great number of texts explaining in detail the qualities of enlightenment so one can tell if someone is enlightened or not. Thrangu Rinpoche and many of the other Tibetan lamas encourage their students to study the *Uttaratantra*, for example, which lays out the qualities and signs of enlightenment. Thrangu Rinpoche has also done an extensive commentary on the *Ornament of Clear Realization* and *Distinguishing the*

Middle from the Extremes which also contain a great deal of information by the Maitreya Buddha on the stages and characteristics of the Buddhist path.

It is difficult to understand how Rechungpa could defy the instructions of Milarepa. We now know that Milarepa is called Tibet's greatest saint, but in Rechungpa's time Milarepa was merely a penniless old man who shunned people and loved to meditate. Rechungpa could not have imagined that Milarepa's biography would become one of the most famous stories in Tibetan Buddhism and that Milarepa's teachings would become the foundation for a lineage which 800 years later would have Dharma centers all over the world.

Due to Rechungpa's great effort we have the Red Chenrezig Practice which is central to the Karmapas, the protector Vajrapani's teachings, the Amitayus practice for long life and health, and the complete Chakrasamvara practice. Chakrasamvara, along with Hevajra and Vajrayogini, are the three main meditational practices of the Kagyu lineage. Without Rechungpa bringing back these practices, it is difficult to imagine the Kagyu path as being complete.

Rechungpa's lack of prominence and lack of a definite lineage of his own was due to the fact that his teachings were absorbed into a number of different lineages: Dusum Khyenpa brought many of Rechungpa's teachings into the Karma Kagyu lineage and the first Drukchen Rinpoche brought Rechungpa's teachings into the Drukpa Kagyu lineage. The first Dzogchen Ponlop Rinpoche and the First Surmong Tulku also incorporated Rechungpa's teachings into their lineages. Rechungpa also had a number of female disciples and one founded the Togdenma tradition made popular by Ani Pelmo's book *Cave in the Snow*.

Thrangu Rinpoche gave the first teachings on Rechungpa in February of 1989 to the Namo Buddha Winter Seminar in Nepal with Peter Roberts translating. Peter Roberts has since written a Ph.D. thesis on Rechungpa. Thrangu Rinpoche later gave a brief teaching on Rechungpa at Karma Dzong in Boulder, Colorado with John Rockwell translating. We have combined these two teachings into one to give a broader biography of the life and practice of Rechungpa.

— Clark Johnson, Ph. D.

Thrangu Rinpoche and His Holiness the Gyalwa Karmapa

Chapter 1

Rechungpa Meets Milarepa

Milarepa, one of Tibet's greatest Buddhist saints, received a prophecy from his guru and also from his *yidam* that he would have two great disciples: one who would be like the sun and the other would be like the moon. The disciple who turned out to be like the sun was Gampopa and the disciple who turned out to be like the moon was Rechungpa.

This biography of Rechungpa shows that he was very intelligent and also that he had a great deal of faith and devotion to the path of Buddhism. However, he didn't always possess this faith. This spiritual biography tells us that although sometimes he was filled with faith for his guru Milarepa, at other times his faith would waver. In the end Rechungpa's faith became strong and he was able to achieve the full fruition of his practice. He achieved Buddhahood as evidenced by the fact that at the time of his death he transformed his elemental body leaving nothing behind.[1]

Spiritual biographies (Tib. *namtar*) are part of the tradition of *Varjayana* Buddhism. They are essentially biographies concerned with how a realized individual first enters the Buddhist path, then how that individual practices on the path, and finally how he or she attains Buddhahood. This biography of Rechungpa is inspirational because it shows what one can do when one is very intelligent and how one progresses along the path with strong exertion as well as what happens when one doesn't have much exertion.

The spiritual biography of Rechungpa is quite long and is composed of three main sections.[2] The first section is brief and deals with Rechungpa's past incarnations. The second section is composed of ten chapters and is concerned with his present life. The third section is also very brief and concerns his future lives. We will skip the first

1

and third sections and concern ourselves with the lifetime in Tibet that helped establish the *Kagyu* lineage.

As a Child Rechungpa Meets Milarepa

This section of the spiritual biography begins by discussing how Rechungpa's birth took place, who his father and mother were, and where and when he was born. In 1083 C.E. he was born at Khab Gunthan and was named Dorje Drag. When he was quite young his father died and his mother married his uncle as was the custom in Tibet. This was very hard economically on the family and Rechungpa. Rechungpa was quite skilled in reading and would go around and recite texts for people and receive offerings. He would then give these offerings to his mother and uncle to supplement the family income.

One day when Rechungpa was eleven years old, he noticed many people gathered at a cave in the valley. Rechungpa went up to this cave and he heard Milarepa inside singing a *spiritual song* (Skt. *doha*). Just hearing this song caused such a transformation in him, he spontaneously experienced great faith. Rechungpa entered the cave. Milarepa was very delighted to see him and began teaching him the *dharma* right away. Milarepa also made a prophecy that in the future, Rechungpa would become a great meditator. Hearing this people said to him, "Oh, how good it would be if you could stay with Milarepa."

Rechungpa then began telling Milarepa about all the hardships he was undergoing and Milarepa replied, "Actually, it seems like you have just a little suffering. I had much greater suffering than that, but I was finally able to meet the great teacher Marpa and receive the oral instructions from him. I then performed great austerities in my practice and finally was able to free myself from all suffering. You too could receive these teachings and practice them and through practicing them be able to attain complete fruition."

Rechungpa did not return to his mother and uncle, but stayed with Milarepa receiving the *upasaka* (layman's vows), the *bodhisatt-*

va vow, and the *Vajrayogini empowerment*. He then began practicing and very positive experiences arose.

Rechungpa's uncle and mother became extremely angry because he had not returned to them, but had instead stayed with Milarepa. So they went and kidnapped Rechungpa by tying him up and taking him away. They then told him, "If you are not going to work reciting for people, then you must work in the fields." So Rechungpa worked in the fields doing very hard labor and through this work he contracted leprosy, a disease of the *nagas*.[3] At that point, Rechungpa's other maternal uncle took great pity on him and said, "Previously, you were like the son of a king and now you have this great suffering. I will take care of you and supply you with food and clothing." His mother and stepfather, however, said to him, "You shouldn't stay here at all. In fact, why don't you just leave the country and go somewhere else."

So Rechungpa went to stay with Milarepa who was living in a cave. While he was there some Indian yogins came to visit. They saw Rechungpa and his leprosy and said, "We see you are very sick. We were planning to go to the Five Peaked Mountain (U Tai Shan) in China. But instead we will return to India, because if you find a very special guru, then you will be cured of this illness."

When Rechungpa went to see Milarepa to request permission to go to India, Milarepa was preparing for a strict retreat. Milarepa gave Rechungpa permission to go and before leaving Rechungpa helped Milarepa build a wall across the opening of his retreat cave.[4]

RECHUNGPA'S FIRST INDIAN TRIP

On the way to India Rechungpa became very, very ill. However, he made it to India where he met an excellent teacher named Balacandra[5] from whom he received the oral instructions of the deity practice of Vajrapani.[6] In just one day of practicing Rechungpa was completely cured of leprosy. This made him extremely happy. He jumped up and started dancing around saying, "I must tell the guru Balacandra that I'm cured." However, this was in the middle of the night so he suddenly realized, "Well, he is sleeping now and if I wake him up, he will probably be very angry at me." He decided not to wake up the guru but to return to Nepal and then to Tibet. This meant leaving without taking the time to request further teachings from Balacandra.

RECHUNGPA'S RETURN TO TIBET

Once Rechungpa returned to Tibet, he started asking around, "Where is Milarepa?" No one seemed to know where he was. Rechungpa then went to the cave where he had left Milarepa and saw that the wall he had helped build was still in place. When he saw this, he thought, "My guru died!" and immediately broke it down and went inside. There was Milarepa meditating and Rechungpa asked Milarepa, "How have you been?" Milarepa sang him a spiritual song saying everything has been going well. His practice had been going well: his meditation was fine, everything was very good. Then he asked, "How did things go with you?"

Rechungpa replied, "I met the guru Balacandra and received the practice of Vajrapani which cured my leprosy. So I am also doing very well."

Rechungpa then received the empowerments and instructions on the *Six Yogas of Naropa* from Milarepa and practiced them. Afterwards he went with Milarepa to Mount Kailash and there through his miraculous powers Milarepa subdued the *Bonpo* master called Naro Bönchung.[7] On witnessing this, Rechungpa said that Milarepa was truly a Buddha and he felt he must practice the instructions that he had received from him. He composed a spiritual song about practicing the instructions of Milarepa. Milarepa, however, said that Rechungpa had to be very careful because there was a great danger of his falling back into *samsara* and into the *disturbing emotions* (Skt. *kleshas*). Milarepa therefore advised him to go and meditate in solitary places. But Rechungpa replied that he had met a great teacher and had received these great instructions so "I am like a garuda flying in the sky and there is no danger of my falling to the ground. I'm like a fish in the water and so there is no danger from waves. With these instructions there is no danger of any obstacles for me." Milarepa replied, "Oh, you are so proud and speak with such great self-confidence that it will be difficult for you to achieve

4

Buddhahood. But I've received this prophecy from Vajrayogini about you so things are bound to turn out well."

Rechungpa decided, "I must stay with Milarepa until I have attained complete realization. Until that occurs, I must stay with him and serve him and receive all the empowerments and *oral instructions*."

However, when the word spread that Rechungpa had been cured of leprosy, his mother and uncle came to Milarepa's cave and demanded Rechungpa return and continue working for them. Milarepa intervened and told them, "If you come any closer, I'm going to cast a spell on you." Rechungpa's uncle and mother became so frightened that they left and never bothered Rechungpa again.[8]

Rechungpa then told Milarepa that his guru in India, Balacandra, had been so kind to him and helped him so much that he wanted to repay his kindness by giving him some gold. He asked Milarepa his opinion and Milarepa said that he should do exactly that. So Rechungpa went around begging and requesting alms. He also received his share of the fields from his mother and his uncle and sold them for gold.

THE SECOND JOURNEY TO INDIA

Rechungpa made his second journey to India with another lama called Ra Lotsawa and another Tibetan teacher called Chiton. Chiton actually means "dog teacher" and he was called this because he had been a hunter and one day while he was out hunting his dog attacked a deer and tore out its entrails. Even though it was wounded and its intestines came out, the deer kept running away. When Chiton saw this, he just couldn't continue being a hunter and instead offered his dog to the monastery and took ordination as a monk.

These three Tibetans left Tibet and came to Nepal which was on the way to India. When they arrived in Nepal, they were requested to give some teachings. A large throne was set up. First Chiton gave the *Dzogchen* dharma teachings. He taught that there are no deities, no demons and so on, teaching from an advanced point of view. The learned Nepalese teachers said, "Oh, Tibetans are no good at teaching dharma. What do they know? How can one visualize a deity in *ngondro* practice and then practice this Dzogchen view of the Varjayana with no deities? These Tibetans obviously don't know what they are doing."[9]

While Rechungpa was in Nepal he met a Nepalese *siddha* named Mondrol Chungpa. Rechungpa asked him, "What is your yidam deity?"[10] The Nepalese siddha replied, "You're not my Guru, so why should I tell you who my yidam is?" That left Rechungpa wondering and so he crept up to the siddha's room to peek in the window to see if he could find out. He found a lot of *thangkas* of many different deities and couldn't figure out which was his yidam deity. Then he bribed one of the siddha's attendants to find out and this attendant told him that Mondrol Chungpa's yidam deity was Vajravarahi. Rechungpa also asked the attendant who his master's teacher was and the attendant told him it was the siddha Tibupa.

Rechungpa then went back to India and found Balacandra and prostrated to him and gave him the offering of gold thanking him for his kindness. Now Balacandra had a lot of power as is illustrated by the following story. One time a woman fainted and remained in a coma and Rechungpa was asked to help her. Rechungpa asked Balacandra to come saying, "Will you be able to revive her?" Balacandra replied, "Yes, I'll be able to bring her back to conscious-ness." Rechungpa thought, "Well, if he can do that, then I must go with him and see this." So he went along with Balacandra and when they got there Balacandra did a fire sadhana. He then picked up the unconscious woman and threw her into the fire. When the uncon-scious woman gained consciousness, Rechungpa developed very great faith and devotion for Balacandra. Rechungpa even drank the dirty water Balacandra washed his hands in as an expression of his great devotion.

In India Rechungpa received meditation instructions on the white, the black, and the multicolored *garuda*. He also received med-itation instruction on the five garudas: the garuda's body, speech, mind, qualities, and activity. After this, Balacandra made a prophecy about Rechungpa. He said that there was a sacred place in the south of Tibet which would be a very good place for him to go and practice because it seemed that Rechungpa practiced the way of a yogi. Balacandra asked him who his teacher was and Rechungpa said that his teacher was Milarepa, a disciple of Marpa and Marpa was a disciple of Naropa. Balacandra replied that it would be very good for Rechungpa to receive teachings from another pupil of Naropa, Tibupa. Now Rechungpa had already given all his gold to Balacandra so he had none left to offer Tibupa. But Balacandra gave Rechungpa a roll of cotton and said, "If you meet Tibupa offer him this." After giving Tibupa the cotton, Rechungpa asked the Tibetan translator who Tibupa's teacher was and so the translator told him the story of Tibupa.

THE STORY OF TIBUPA

Tibupa's father was called in Tibetan "laughing vajra" and his mother was called Samantabhadra and they had three sons. Tibupa was the oldest and when he was thirteen years old, he died. This caused his parents great suffering and unhappiness. They took him to the cemetery and when he was laid down, a pigeon flew down to where the body was, bent its head down three times and died. As soon as the pigeon died, Tibupa came back to life. The people who worked carrying dead bodies to the cemetery became very frightened and said, "This body has been invaded by a zombie spirit"[11] Actually the mind that had entered the body was that of Dharmadode, Marpa's son.[12]

Being the son of Marpa he had learned some of the Indian language of that part of India and said, "Don't be frightened. I'm not a zombie. I'm just a body that has come back to life. It's safe for you to take me home." So his parents were overjoyed and took him back home and everyone was very amazed. They said, "He's died and now he's come back again." Some people thought that he had been protected by prayers for the continuation of his life. His parents were very happy to have him living with them again, but after being with him for a time, they noticed that their son was much calmer than before, that he had more respect for his parents and was more interested in the dharma. They gradually realized this was not actually their son so they asked him, "Well, who are you?" Tibupa explained that he had received the practice of *phowa trongchub* from his father

Marpa. This phowa practice allows one to transfer one's consciousness out of one's body into the body of a corpse.

Marpa had seven sons but only Dharmadode was a good dharma practitioner. Dharmadode's ability to help others made him very special to Marpa. Much earlier Naropa had predicted that there would be an obstacle for him and Dharmadode would have to do an intensive retreat and accumulate mantras to overcome the obstacle. While Dharmadode was in retreat an obstacle arose. One day there was a great celebration taking place in the neighborhood. Dharmadode thought, "I have a well-known father and mother. I am also young and if old people can go to this fair, I should also be able to go. Marpa told him to stay in retreat but Dharmadode insisted. So Marpa consented by saying, "If you go to the fair you must obey these three commands, 'First, do not sit in the front row. Second, do not teach the dharma at the fair and third, do not drink any alcohol.'"

When Dharmadode went to the fair, he began by sitting in the back row. Once he had sat down everyone else saw him and said, "Oh, there is Marpa's son. By all means you must sit up front. You can't sit in back so please come and sit up front. Then everyone asked him to teach the dharma and kept insisting until Dharmadode was forced to teach the dharma. After he had taught, everyone said, "This is a great celebration, you must have something to drink." Dharmadode could not refuse and so he had something to drink and became a little drunk.

When he was riding a horse home, he fell off his horse and broke his head open against a rock. Dharmadode knew he would not recover, but he had mastered the practice of the ejection and transference of consciousness. He would have to find another body,[13] but his pupils couldn't find another body. All they could find was a dead pigeon. So they brought the dead pigeon and Marpa acting as his guru told his son in a command prophesy, "You should eject and transfer your consciousness into this pigeon. You should then fly to India to the Cool Grove charnel ground where you will find a corpse of a young boy. Transfer your consciousness into that body so that you will be able to benefit many sentient beings with your teachings." He then flew from Tibet down to India where he found Tibupa's body and transferred his consciousness into it. The Indian name for a pigeon is "tibu" and this is how he became known as Tibupa.

When Tibupa met Naropa, Naropa did a miracle in which he rose into space and danced there. In the rainbow light of this manifestation Tilopa appeared and said to him, "You are the son of Marpa, you are Tibupa, and so you have the blessing of Naropa." He then said, "Your name in India is Tibupa, but because you have had many *tantric teachings*, you should be called "the tree of mantras" or *Sang Dongpo* in Tibetan.

Rechungpa went off to find this Tibupa and eventually he found him, saying, "I've gone through a lot of difficulties to get here: I've come through extremely cold places, through areas infested by illness, and through burning hot places. Ignoring all these dangers, I've come to you to receive dharma teachings. So with your great compassion please give me all the dharma teachings you have."

Tibupa felt very pleased with him and said, "Oh, he has obviously meditated a lot and is very intelligent." But Tibupa had a Tibetan translator with him who said, "No, he's just giving you an expected introduction." Tibupa then decided he had better check to see whether Rechungpa was genuine or pretending. So he asked him, "What's your lineage? What kind of instructions do you need?" Rechungpa then sang a spiritual song explaining that his lineage came from Tilopa through Naropa and Milarepa and that he had come to seek out five of the nine dakini teachings. When he said that, Tibupa became very happy and said, "This is a genuine person. He's not trying to deceive me." He said, "I will give you all the instructions one by one."

Rechungpa thought that he must practice the same yidam as Tibupa. He asked the teacher, "Do you have a yidam?" and the teacher said, "Yes, of course." Rechungpa asked who the yidam was and Tibupa replied, "I'm not going to tell you, it's my commitment to keep it secret so I can't tell you." Rechungpa began thinking about how he was going to find out what Tibupa's yidam was. This guru had his bedroom and Rechungpa had his separate place to sleep. At some point in the night, the guru got up and started reciting mantras. Rechungpa listened very carefully trying to make them out, but couldn't make out anything more than a couple of HUMs. So he thought he should get closer. He got out of his bedclothes and with nothing on crept much closer. But now he was feeling very frightened and couldn't hear the mantra over his own heavy breathing. When the guru finished reciting his mantra, he could see Rechungpa there and said, "Oh, Tibetan, what's the matter with you? Have you gone insane? Why are you wandering about at night with nothing on?" Rechungpa replied, "Well, actually I've been trying to work out what your yidam is, so I was creeping up here to try to make out what the mantra was." The guru said, "You're a very clever Tibetan and very intelligent," and they both had a good laugh.

During his stay, Tibupa went through the teachings although Rechungpa wasn't able to translate them himself. There were other translators there who translated the teachings for him and so in this way Rechungpa obtained all of the teachings of the formless dakinis and began practicing them.[14]

When Rechungpa began this return to Tibet, he met another Indian teacher called Mirti who had the "fast feet instruction" which is the meditation on how to walk very quickly. He received these instructions and mastered them and was thus able to walk from India to Tibet in only six days.[15] Also on the way he met many other teachers and received the Dzogchen instructions and the instructions on two other yidam deities.

Chapter 2

Rechungpa's Third Journey to India

After receiving the oral instructions from Tibupa, Rechungpa arrived in Tibet. When he met Milarepa and told him of all of the teachings he had received, Milarepa was very delighted. Milarepa then gave Rechungpa the instructions on the Six Yogas of Naropa and the instructions on Mahamudra practice. Rechungpa practiced these teachings very diligently and special realization arose in him.

MILAREPA'S ENCOUNTER WITH THE LOGICIANS

Rechungpa was staying with Milarepa who by this time had become very famous. One day there were two very learned monks who started slandering Milarepa by saying, "This Milarepa doesn't know anything at all about the dharma and so he shouldn't be teaching it. We should debate Milarepa and thereby show what he is and have him expelled from the country." These two monks called Dallo and Loden came to Milarepa and said, "All these people have great faith in you and therefore you must have some very great qualities and be very learned. We therefore should like to have a discussion about the dharma with you."

They began by asking Milarepa, "What sort of dharma do you know and who is your guru?" So Milarepa sang to them a spiritual song about his lineage and what practices he was doing and so forth. The monks said, "Well, you might fool the ordinary people by singing songs. However, we are very educated individuals, so don't sing songs to us. We have to engage in a serious discussion about the dharma." Milarepa said, "I practice on the *subtle winds* and the *subtle channels* (Skt. *prana* and *nadi*)." They said, "Oh, this is not very important at all. Fish in the water can do without air, and even animals that hibernate underground can do without breathing, so this is not rare or special." They then asked Milarepa to explain his understanding of the ten *perfections* (Skt. *paramitas*). So Milarepa sang a spiritual song about his understanding of these perfections. The two educated monks had to admit, "Well, it looks like you understand that. However, the perfections are not the most important aspect of dharma. Most important is being well trained in logical reasoning. So, in terms of logic, it is very important that you show us the conditions or the reasons things are in contradiction to each other, the way things are connected to each other, and the way things are inseparable from each other." Milarepa said, "Oh, of course! An example of a contradiction is that your mind and the dharma are in contradiction. An example of inseparability is that your mind and the disturbing emotions are inseparably connected."

The monks then said, "Well, it doesn't help to banter about bad words. What you need to do is to establish definitions."

So Milarepa replied, "According to your understanding, is space something that is obstructing or is it something non-obstructing?" The second logician said, "That is no problem. The Buddha has clearly said that space is not obstructing and besides there is no one who has ever said that space obstructs." Then Milarepa through the miraculous power of his meditative concentration made the space around the monks such that they could no longer move. "Space is obstructing, isn't it?" he said. "Is this rock obstructing or is it non-obstructing?" Again through the power of his meditative concentration, he ran in and out of the rock saying, "It's unobstructing, isn't it?"[16]

At this point the monks were speechless. However, they finally said, "Unless we engage in some kind of dharma discussion, this is totally pointless." One monk had absolutely no faith in Milarepa and the other thought, "This Milarepa is very strange." They then returned home, but the one who was doubtful entered his home and found the Tibetan painting (a thangka) of the Buddha that was hanging in his house had fallen so that the Buddha was upside down which is a very bad omen. He later returned to Milarepa's cave and as soon as he came in Milarepa said, "It's one thing if your mind doesn't follow the dharma properly, but please don't be disrespectful to the

Buddha." After hearing this the monk went back to his other friend and said, "This Milarepa is very strange and hasn't studied much dharma. Nevertheless, we have studied a lot of dharma and it hasn't tamed our mind very much, while this Milarepa has tamed his mind." The monk lacking faith continued, "That is not true at all. It is complete nonsense."

MILAREPA'S WARNING

All during this time Rechungpa observed and thought, "My guru displayed some wonderful miracles, but he didn't do very well in the debate. These are very poor dharma practitioners and so I should go back and study logic and debate so I can defeat them in debate. Milarepa knows black magic, but he won't teach it to me." Rechungpa then asked Milarepa if he could go to India a third time.

Milarepa said to Rechungpa, "Don't go to India to study logic and sorcery. This is just worldly thinking and even if you learn sorcery and logic, it will not lead to Buddhahood. The best thing for you to do is just to stay here and practice and meditate." But Rechungpa said he really had to go to India and there's no way he would stay. So Milarepa said, "If you really have to go to India then don't go there to study logic and sorcery, but go to receive meditation instructions and practice." Milarepa said that he had received teachings from Marpa that had come from Tilopa and Naropa who received them from the *dakinis*. There were nine dharma teachings that had been given by the dakinis. Milarepa had only received four of these teachings because Marpa had been able to bring only four back to Tibet. Marpa had told Milarepa, "I've taught you four dakini teachings and there are still five in India. So if you can go to India, even though you are not able to meet Naropa, you can meet someone in his lineage who has received these teachings. If these other five dakini teachings come to Tibet, it will be very auspicious." Milarepa could have gotten these teachings but he felt very satisfied with practicing Mahamudra and the Six Yogas of Naropa. He really enjoyed doing meditation so he couldn't bear to leave his meditation and go off to India. Having spent so much time in meditation, he was now too old

13

to go to India. Milarepa said to Rechungpa, "But you're young and intelligent and diligent, so if you go to India it will be very good if you can receive the remaining five dakini teachings and bring them to Tibet." Then Milarepa and Rechungpa exchanged what they had for gold and Milarepa said to Rechungpa one last time, "If you go to India and study logic and sorcery, it will just defile your mind and create more disturbing emotions causing you to move backward on the path. Instead seek out and receive these teachings of the formless dakinis."

Rechungpa traveled to India a third time and was able to meet Tibupa again. From Tibupa he received all the nine teachings on the formless dakini lineage.

HOW RECHUNGPA RECEIVED THE LONG LIFE PRACTICE OF AMITAYUS

One day Tibupa told Rechungpa that he should go into town and take a look around. So Rechungpa went off to see what this town was like. On the way he passed a very tall, thin yogi who took a very good look at Rechungpa and said, "What a very sweet handsome young Tibetan you are, but it is a shame you've only got seven days to live." This gave Rechungpa a fright and he thought, "I've got only seven days left. What am I going to do?" He went running straight back to Tibupa and told him, "I've just met a yogi in the street and he's told me I've only got a week to live. What shall I do?" Tibupa asked Rechungpa, "Are you that afraid of dying?" and Rechungpa replied, "Well, actually I'm not very frightened of dying, but I've gone through a lot of trouble to come down to India and receive these teachings of the formless dakinis. If I die here, it will all be completely meaningless. I've got to take these teachings back to Tibet and give them to Milarepa."

Tibupa then said, "Actually I knew you didn't have very long to live, so I told you to go into town. I knew you would meet this person who told you that you didn't have long to live. But there's no need to be afraid of dying because there is this woman called Machig Drupay Gyalmo (which means 'one mother, the queen of accomplishment') living in a cave. Machig Drupay Gyalmo has achieved the practice of long life and is five-hundred years old, but she looks like a sixteen-year-old girl." He told Rechungpa to go see her and so Rechungpa went to her cave, met her, gave offerings, and prostrated to her.

She said, "Well, what do you want?" He said, "I've been to town and I've met this yogi who told me I only have a week to live. So please give me the *siddhi* of long life." Then Machig Drupay Gyalmo asked Rechungpa, "Can you do without sleep for a week?" and he replied, "Yes, I can." She then gave him this long-life practice to do and he did it continuously night and day for seven days. At the end of seven days, he had a vision of Amitayus who taught him the long-life sadhana in a long form, a middle form, and a short form.

After this Machig Drupay Gyalmo asked him how long he wanted to live and Rechungpa replied, "I want to live until I don't want to live anymore." She asked how old he was now and he said he was forty-two. She said, "You wicked Tibetan with such a great desire to live so long. Your teacher Milarepa is now eighty-three and is going to live until his eighty-fourth year so you can do the same." Then Rechungpa received from Machig Drupay Gyalmo the empowerment and transmission and instructions for the Red Chenrezig Practice.[17] One night after receiving this empowerment he had many dreams and one of these dreams was a *pandita* dancing in the sky. Then it began to rain flowers and in the midst of this rain of flowers were dakinis who said that he had received a very good empowerment and had practiced it well. They sang a song to him. Rechungpa thought the song sounded so beautiful, he paid very close attention to the wonderful melody. When he woke up, he realized that he didn't know what the words of the song were. All he could remember was just one line and this line had been written on Tibupa's doorway.

Rechungpa received many other instructions from Tibupa and Machig Drupay Gyalmo and these teachings were translated into Tibetan. Tibupa said that the translation was not perfect, he didn't really know how to translate it completely correctly. He made the prophecy that it didn't matter because in the future other people would go through and remove the mistakes in the translation.

After having received the oral instructions on Amitayus,

Rechungpa returned to Balacandra. Balacandra then asked Rechungpa, "Did you meet Tibupa? Did you receive good teaching? Did you develop great faith in him?" Rechungpa replied, "Yes, I met the teacher and he's a very great and special teacher. I have great faith in him and received teachings and instructions from him."

But then Rechungap went and studied black magic and also logic. The result of this was that he became more arrogant and proud.

RECHUNGPA'S RETURN

Before returning to Tibet, Rechungpa first went to Nepal and met a Nepalese siddha who asked him, "What happened to you? Did everything go well? Were you able to travel to India without any problem? What teachers did you meet and what instructions did you get?" Rechungpa replied, "I met the teachers Tibupa and Machig Drupay Gyalmo and had no problems traveling through India and I received many instructions." He then showed this Nepalese siddha his texts. When the Nepalese examined them, he said, "Well, they haven't been translated very correctly, but I'll go through them and correct errors in the translation."

So the Nepalese siddha did that, making Tibupa's prophecy come true that someone would remove the errors in translation. Rechungpa also received many special teachings and instructions from this siddha.

On the way back to Tibet he also met a woman who was an emanation of a *dakini*,[18] who removed the rest of the mistakes from his translation. Afterwards, he met a nonBuddhist sorcerer from whom he received teachings on the practice of mantras that can do harm to others. By the time he returned to Tibet he had developed the obstacle of great pride.

Chapter 3

Milarepa Tames Rechungpa

When Rechungpa returned from his third journey to India, Milarepa was in retreat in a cave in an area called Tramar Chonglong which means the "red cliffs of the chameleon valley." Milarepa was meditating in this valley and thought, "My pupil, Rechungpa, has gone to India. I wonder when he's coming back and how he is." So he rested in *samadhi* and had a vision of Rechungpa returning from India as a crystal *stupa* shining with light indicating that he had received these teachings. This shining light was coming closer and closer to the Tibetan border. But then, when Rechungpa met this nonBuddhist who practiced sorcery, the stupa of light was transformed into a wild dust-blowing tempest of wind as he approached Tibet. Milarepa thought, "This is not good. An obstacle has occurred." And so he decided he must break his retreat. Milarepa flew from where he was to the area of Nyantang in Tibet. The footprints of where Milarepa landed can still be found there in the rock.

So, while Rechungpa was returning he went through an area of Tibet called Gungtang and reached the area called Palmo Paltang which is a great empty plain. Milarepa came to meet him there and as they were approaching each other on this plain, they could see each other coming. Rechungpa thought, "I've been to India three times and I've met with great teachers such as Tibupa. This time I've received very special meditation instructions. So I'm not the same as I was before I went to India." Rechungpa was feeling proud and remembered Milarepa had said that the instructions of the formless dakinis were very special and important. He thought, "I've been to India and possess these instructions." He began wondering if Milarepa was going straight to him when they met. He thought, "Yes, he'll probably come straight to me."

Milarepa saw Rechungpa coming and thought, "Oh, he's become very proud, this isn't good!" So he went and sat on a big boulder and when Rechungpa arrived he said, "So you've come back from India. I see this has not been such a great thing. All the siddhas and all the dakinis of India come to me for teachings. So you should prostrate to me and treat me with respect." Rechungpa had brought a sandalwood staff from India which Tibupa had given him to take to Tibet so he offered this to Milarepa respectfully and prostrated to him. While doing this he thought, "Well, I prostrated to him first, he's probably going to prostrate to me now." But Milarepa just sat there and didn't prostrate to him. So Rechungpa got upset about this and thought, "He's not treating me very well!" Then he asked Milarepa, "How have you been while I've been in India? How are all the other yogis? Have you been in good health and where have you been?"

Milarepa thought to himself, "Oh he's very proud now that he's received the instructions of this sorcery. That's what has caused this." So Milarepa started laughing and he sang a spiritual song to Rechungpa. In his song Milarepa said that he had eliminated the sickness of the five disturbing emotions. Now he is in good health and free of the ripening of karma, thus completely free. He has perfect health and due to the kindness of Marpa he's realized that samsara and *nirvana* are just mind and therefore he has no problems or difficulties at all. And all the other yogis were well and meditating in solitude.

Then Milarepa asked Rechungpa, "How was your journey to India and did you get good instructions?" Rechungpa replied, "Yes, I have received good instructions." Milarepa then asked, "Have you returned from India with these instructions without any pride?" Rechungpa said, "Well, I've received the instructions of the formless dakinis to which you attach such great importance. So for others to respect these teachings and realize they are important, you also have to treat these teachings with great respect and treat them as having great value." He then gave the texts that he'd brought back from India to Milarepa.

To break Rechungpa's pride, Milarepa took these texts and Tibupa's sandalwood staff and began to run at very great speed.

Rechungpa had to run behind him and Rechungpa was having such a hard time keeping up that he sang to Milarepa a spiritual song describing what a difficult time he was having keeping up with him.

So Milarepa stopped, sat down, and sang a spiritual song in return. Then they walked on together. But as they were going along Rechungpa thought, "If this were some other lama, I would have had a very great welcome and been treated very well upon my return from India with all these instructions. But my lama has nothing except this body which is in very poor condition and he has only his clothes which are also in very poor condition. So what kind of a welcome can I expect from someone like that?" Then Rechungpa thought, "Having had these instructions from India I just can't practice these in poverty and hardship. I have to do my meditation practice in wealth and prosperity and in pleasant circumstances." Milarepa knew he was thinking these bad thoughts. As they were walking along on this plain, there was a yak horn lying on the ground. Milarepa told Rechungpa to pick up the yak horn and bring it with him. Rechungpa thought, "My lama is always saying we mustn't have any possessions or wealth and then he becomes really attached to this little yak horn. This horn is of no use to anyone." He said to Milarepa, "This yak horn is not going to be of any use, so let's just leave it behind."

But Milarepa said, "The yak horn is good: we don't have to develop any attachment to it, and it might come in handy sometime." So Rechungpa picked up the horn and they both walked along the plain of Palmo Paltang which is a very great, completely flat, deserted plain. Nothing is there, no shelter or anything.

Then clouds began to gather in the sky and a hailstorm arose with a very fierce wind. Rechungpa became very cold and had no time to look around and see what was happening to Milarepa. He just lay down and covered himself with his cotton robe and felt very cold. When the hail began, he looked around and there was no sign of Milarepa anywhere. Then he thought he heard a voice coming from the yak horn. He looked up and down and all over but there was still no sign of Milarepa anywhere. So he thought, "Well I'd better take this yak horn along because Milarepa wants it." But when he tried to pick it up he couldn't because it was too heavy. He looked inside the yak horn and Milarepa was sitting inside.

Milarepa was sitting in there very comfortably with plenty of space. He hadn't gotten any smaller and the yak horn hadn't gotten any bigger, but he was quite comfortable. He said to Rechungpa, "If your powers are any good, you come in here as well. It's so nice in here without any hail or wind!" Rechungpa thought, "Well why not?" But he couldn't even get his hand into the yak horn. This didn't develop faith in Milarepa. He just thought, "Well, I don't know the kinds of sorcery Milarepa can do, but what I know for sure is he's very good at creating hailstorms." The sun began to shine and Rechungpa's cotton robes were all wet. So he laid them out to dry. Milarepa said to him, "You needn't have gone all the way to India to learn sorcery because I know sorcery and you could have learned it from me. But I'm just satisfied with the Six Yogas of Naropa and Mahamudra and so I didn't have any wish to go to India. Your going to India and receiving instructions on the formless dakinis is very good."

Rechungpa said, "But I'm hungry and cold. Let's go begging for alms." Milarepa replied, "Now is not the time to go begging for food. It's time to meditate." So Rechungpa said to him, "The time to go begging for food is when you are hungry and I'm hungry now, so this is the time to go begging for food."

There were some nomadic families on the plain. It was very cold and so they went to these families and Rechungpa said to Milarepa, "We must beg from a small family in a small tent." But Milarepa said, "Oh no, they won't give us any alms. But if that is where you intend to go begging then you go and beg there." So Rechungpa went to this little tent to beg and an old woman came out and began telling him off with, "You yogis come in the morning and you come in the evening begging for food. You don't do any work and all you think about is getting food to eat. I've already given away what I had to give this morning so there's nothing left for you. Just go away!" And so Milarepa said to Rechungpa, "I think we'd better not have anything to eat this evening. I think it's better we go now and get some sleep." So they went a little distance away and laid down to sleep. In the middle of the night they heard sounds and shouting from the camp. In the morning when they woke up, all the nomadic families had left except for the one yak skin tent that belonged to the old woman.

20

When they went back to the tent, they found that the old woman had died and in the tent there was a lot of *tsampa* (dried barley), cheese, and yogurt. So Milarepa said, "This is impermanence. Last night she wouldn't give us any of her food and today all this food is ours to eat." They divided up the food and Rechungpa said that they should eat some and carry some with them. When they finished Rechungpa said, "So, let's go!" but Milarepa said, "No, we've eaten the food of a dead person and now we have to do something for her. So you carry the dead body over there." Rechungpa protested, "Oh! This is a really disgusting body and it's so dirty!" But he had no choice and with great disgust carried the body to where Milarepa wanted it. Then Milarepa did the *phowa* transference of consciousness for her.[19]

MILAREPA CONTINUES TO TAME RECHUNGPA

Milarepa then said, "Now we should go to somewhere like Mt. Kailash and Mt. Lachi, which are very solitary, so we can meditate there." Rechungpa disagreed, "Oh no! I'm very tired and weak. We need to go somewhere where people are living and I can rest. It won't do to go to some uninhabited place in the condition I'm in." So Milarepa did as Rechungpa said and they went to an inhabited area where Rechungpa said, "Now we need to find a particular sponsor, someone to look after us." Milarepa said, "No, let's go to the first tent we see, someone we don't know at all." They did and Milarepa said, "Now I need some water so you go and get me some water and I'll light a fire. There's some water nearby and there's also some a long way off, but the water nearby doesn't suit me, it's bad for my health. Go and get me the water that's a long way off."

Rechungpa went to get the water in a sort of narrow valley, but then everything began to change and the narrow valley seemed to change into a plain. Then a *kyang* (a wild ass of Tibet) approached and the kyang gave birth to another and the newborn gave birth to another one. Each one kept giving birth to a new one, so there were a hundred of these new young kyangs running about and playing. Rechungpa became very distracted watching this and thought, "This is quite amazing! Kyangs usually live out on the plains, not in narrow canyons with cliffs and forests and they don't usually give birth so quickly!" He watched these things in fascination until a wolf eventually appeared and the kyangs ran far away. Then Rechungpa thought, "Oh, I've spent a long time doing this and I haven't gotten the water. I must get back quickly, otherwise Milarepa will be telling me off!"

Meanwhile, Milarepa was sitting in meditation and praying to the dakinis. Milarepa invoked the dakinis in front of him. He took Rechungpa's container of texts and requested that the dakinis take up with them all the teachings having to do with the formless dakini teachings and to throw down to the ground all the teachings on logic and black magic. Saying this the dakini teachings went up and everything else fell to earth. Milarepa then took these and threw them into the fire.

As Rechungpa was returning, he could smell burning paper. He thought, "Well, that's very strange, why do I smell burning paper?" When he got back, he went to the container his texts had been in and found it empty. Then he thought, "My lama has become jealous of me! I've visited India and developed all these great qualities. I've learned all these profound instructions and now he's so envious of me he burned my texts!" So he went up to Milarepa and said to him, "Where are my texts?" Milarepa replied, "You've been gone so long I didn't think you were ever coming back. I thought you were probably dead. I'm just a meditator and for me texts would just be a distraction and cause an obstacle so I used them for the fire."

Rechungpa became very upset and thought, "Maybe I'll go back to Tibupa or I'll go traveling around to other places in Tibet. I'm not going to stay here with Milarepa, it's no good!" He lost all his faith in Milarepa and said to him, "Well, all that I've done is completely worthless; all the gold that I had, all the hardships that I had going to India and getting all these instructions are all for nothing. So I'm not going to stay here. I'm going off to travel around parts of Tibet." Milarepa replied, "You don't need to lose faith in me. I know you've been enjoying watching these *kyangs* but they are just animals; they're not really anything much worth looking at. I'll give you something worth looking at." Then on top of Milarepa's head appeared a throne on which was seated Marpa and beside his right ear appeared the sun and by his left ear the moon. Then from his nostrils shone the light rays of five colors and on his tongue appeared an eight-petaled lotus with the Sanskrit vowels and consonants on it and from his heart appeared the knot of eternity.

Milarepa sang Rechungpa a song saying, "Above my head is Marpa. He is inseparable from Vajradhara and he has a very pro-found, superior and exceptional lineage. By my right and left ear are the sun and the moon. This is a sign of the inseparability of means and wisdom, of *upaya* and *prajna*. From my nostrils radiate light rays of five different colors. This is a result of my having such complete control of the subtle winds[20] (Tib. *lung*) of my body, but they've all entered into the central channel. And at my heart there's the knot of eternity which shows that I have attained the complete wisdom of the Buddha's mind. So, kyangs are just animals and not worth looking at. This, however, is something that is worth looking at. This has great meaning."

Even though Milarepa sang this song to Rechungpa, Rechungpa's faith in Milarepa did not return. Rechungpa said, "Well, if you are such a great lama and perform great miracles, bring me my texts back. If you don't, I will still be very disappointed with you!" So Rechungpa was feeling unhappy and just sat down and put his elbow on his knee, resting his head against his hand and whistling to himself, shaking his leg, and generally being very displeased and unhappy. Consequently, Milarepa created another miracle by making himself transparent so one could see there was *Chakrasamvara* in his heart, *Hevajra* in his navel, in his throat was the *Mahamaya* and a *Guhyasamaja* at the crown of his head. Milarepa said, "Now look! This is a miracle that is really worth looking at!" And Rechungpa said, "This is a good miracle, but I'm still unhappy about my texts."

There was a great big rock nearby and Milarepa got on top of it and started riding it like a horse. He was riding around back and forth on this great big rock when he went into the sky with fire and water coming out of his body. He was singing a song to Rechungpa saying,

"This fire blazing out of my body is a sign of having attained the *samadhi of great exhaustion*, the exhaustion of negativity." Rechungpa replied, "Now your miracles are becoming like a child playing and are just irritating me. What I want are my books! Give me back my books!"

Then Milarepa started flying up into the sky and was gliding in the sky just like a vulture. Sometimes he would come swooping down very fast and then he'd go flying up high very fast. He sang a song to Rechungpa saying, "There are not many people who can fly like this! This flying is due to the power of the dharma." But Rechungpa wouldn't even look at him so Milarepa started flying higher and higher in the sky until he became invisible. Eventually Rechungpa looked up and saw that he was gone without any trace. He thought, "Oh, my lama has obviously flown away to the pure realms! What can I do without a lama? I lost faith in him and I've been unpleasant towards him and he's such a very special lama! Now he's gone to the pure realms and that is something I can't do. I can't follow him. I must be crazy, I've made a very big mistake!"

Rechungpa was full of remorse and thought, "I'm going to kill myself!" So he ran to the edge of a cliff and jumped off, but he found himself falling very slowly. He could feel and smell Milarepa. He looked up from the bottom and he could not only see Milarepa, he could see three Milarepas standing there on the cliff. He asked Milarepa to forgive him saying, "I confess, I've been wrong. Please forgive me and give me dharma teachings!"

The three Milarepas replied to him at the same time, "But to which Milarepa are you going to confess? Which one are you going to have faith in? Which one are you going to receive dharma instructions from?" And Rechungpa said, "I'm going to confess to the middle one and I'm going to trust and request teachings from the middle Milarepa."

So Rechungpa returned with Milarepa to the cave and Milarepa said, "I sent you to India to get these very special instructions but you also learned instructions in sorcery. For instructions in sorcery you can't get any more powerful than the ones I have. But by using them

I accumulated very bad karma and experienced a lot of difficulty in purifying myself. So I decided to ignore the sorcery and just receive and practice instructions which will bring about the attainment of Buddhahood. It is my hope that you will achieve Buddhahood within one lifetime so I was worried that with these texts you would become a sorcerer or someone who just teaches from texts while not doing any practice. For that reason I burned the texts on sorcery and logic, but I haven't burned the texts on the instructions of the formless dakinis."

Then Milarepa recited a prayer and from an opening in the rocks there appeared the pages with the instructions of the formless dakinis. They just fell out from the rocks. When Rechungpa saw that he thought, "My lama really is the Buddha and so I must stay with him and must practice his teachings. For twelve years I will be his attendant, for twelve years I will receive his teachings, for twelve years I will practice with him." And so he made that very firm and very complete commitment. This is how Milarepa was able to eliminate the obstacle of pride that had arisen in Rechungpa.[21]

There is excellent instructions in these stories of Rechungpa which is that we have to be free of the mind's busyness and be free of pride. If we have pride, we can't develop faith and devotion for the lama and the dharma. Without this we won't be able to practice fully. We have to be able to eliminate the mind poisons to develop faith and devotion so that we will be able to practice well.

Tilopa

Tilopa was born in India a little over 1,000 years ago. He was an emanation of Chakrasamvara. He was a simple cowherd who later became a king. Yet, he grew weary of royalty and took up meditation and living as a wandering yogi. His most famous student was Naropa who learned the vajrayana path from him and later transmitted these teachings to Marpa.

Chapter 4

Milarepa Prepares Rechungpa for the Lineage

Rechungpa had gone to India where he received very special instructions and teachings, but developed an obstacle in the form of pride. To eliminate that pride, Milarepa created all sorts of miracles and burned Rechungpa's texts on logic and sorcery. Pride is a very powerful obstacle but it doesn't arise when one has difficulties and suffering. Pride arises when things are going very well. When one is having difficulties and suffering, it is the disturbing emotions such as anger and ignorance that arise. It was when everything seemed to be going well that Rechungpa developed excessive pride.

There was a group of pupils called *nyamas* in Tibetan. Nyamas are dharma students who engage in their daily activities but on the new and full moon days they come to see a teacher and receive teachings and practice. The new moon day is called "*nyamkong*" and this is where they get their name from. These people assembled and said, "Rechungpa was sent to India to receive special instructions in sorcery and in logical debate." So they asked Rechungpa how things had gone. Rechungpa sang a song in reply:

I have met my teacher Milarepa who is a Buddha and I have received special instructions from the oral lineage. I have also received the instructions of the formless dakinis so I am very fortunate. Additionally, I practiced the contemplation of the view, meditation, and conduct.

27

My teacher Milarepa told me that the ultimate view is the view of the union of emptiness and wisdom, but he warned that we could develop the view purely on the intellectual level and thus be able to express this view only through words. This is the conceptual view, not the understanding of the true meaning.

What we need to do is to become certain of the meaning of the view by directly experiencing the mind itself thus liberating ourselves from the disturbing emotions. From that experience we gain complete conviction of the meaning of the view.

In meditation we need to have *luminosity* and the absence of fixation or clinging. In meditation we just rest in mental stability and peace of mind. But be warned that our meditation could get lost in this feeling of calmness. Mental stability by itself will not give us liberation, so we need to have luminosity for the *five wisdoms* to arise in meditation.

If our mind is dull or agitated, these five wisdoms will not be able to develop. So we have to remove dullness and agitation in our meditation. When we are meditating, we have to have mindfulness and awareness to free us from attachment and clinging.

There is the danger of falling into undisciplined behavior so our conduct should support the view of meditation. We therefore need to have mindfulness, awareness, and self-control at all times. Our conduct should be free of any attachment and this will result in stainless, unsurpassable conduct.

But be warned that we will attain signs and omens of achievement and recognizing these, we will feel so pleased and become attached to these signs thinking, "Now things are going very well." This attachment prevents the attainment of our goal, enlightenment. So to attain enlightenment we must overcome and eliminate the disturbing emotions.

Milarepa who was listening to this told Rechungpa that his going to India to receive the profound instructions and bringing them back was very good. This would be very beneficial in the future for many beings. He then asked Rechungpa for the instructions of the formless dakinis that he had brought back from India. Rechungpa said that in addition to these, he had received the long-life practice from Machig Drupay Gyalmo and asked Milarepa if he wanted this as well. Milarepa said, "'Giving us these teachings would be very good! I do not need to have this long life practice for myself because I am an old man. But you're young, so if you give me the long-life practice of Machig Drupay Gyalmo for the lineage that would be very good." Then Rechungpa gave Milarepa the instructions of the formless dakinis and the long-life practice which Milarepa later taught to Gampopa. In this way these practices have been passed on and continued and have spread. Rechungpa stayed on with Milarepa as his attendant and he was inseparable from him.

Gampopa Also Becomes Milarepa's Student

One day Milarepa sang a song saying that Gampopa was going to come to see him and that Gampopa would benefit many beings in the future. When Gampopa arrived, Milarepa gave him meditation instructions. Then one day Milarepa told Gampopa and Rechungpa and the yogi Repa Shiwao to examine their dreams that night to see what the future held in store for them. They should come and tell him their dreams and Milarepa would tell them whether there was a good or a bad omen in them.

Early next morning the first person to arrive was Repa Shiwao who was very happy. "I had a very good dream last night. I dreamt that in the East the sun rose and the sun merged into my heart." Later Rechungpa came and said, "I had a dream, but I don't know what it meant. I dreamt I went to three valleys and in each one I shouted very loudly three times."[22] Then Gampopa came and was very depressed and he said, "I had a terrible dream!" But Milarepa said, "Tell me the dream and I'll tell you whether it's a good or bad one." So Gampopa said, "I dreamt that I killed all kinds of people and I was going around cutting their heads off and other things. This is very, very bad. So

29

please give me some kind of method to purify myself." At that, Milarepa took hold of his hand and said, "This is an incredibly good dream! I had very great hopes for you and it seems that things will go as I'd hoped. You will greatly benefit the dharma in the future: you will have many students, and you will be my principal disciple."

Then he said that Shiwao's dream was not a very good dream, because it showed that he had very limited motivation and not much *bodhichitta*. He had more of a *shravaka* motivation. The dream of seeing the sunrise merging into his heart showed that his practice would go very well, but he wouldn't benefit anyone else. "You're not much benefit to anyone else now and you won't benefit many beings in the future. But you're going to go to a pure realm." About Rechungpa's dream, he said that going to three valleys and shouting three times was a sign of disobeying the guru three times. "I told you not to go to India and you went. Then I told you not to study sorcery and logic and you went ahead and studied sorcery and logic. It looks like one more time you are going to disobey me. In a future lifetime you will become a very great teacher, a very great spiritual friend to people." Milarepa had a prophecy from *Vajravarahi* (Tib. Dorje Phagmo) which said that the instructions of the oral lineage were like a jewel and this jewel was in the center of Milarepa's heart. In this prophecy Vajravarahi said that if he took this jewel out of his heart and placed it on the head of Dorje Drakpa (Rechungpa) then there would be a very great result. Therefore Milarepa transmitted the instructions to his pupil who was like the sun, Gampopa, and to his pupil who was like the moon, Rechungpa, and gradually passed on these instructions to all of his pupils who were like the stars.

Milarepa gave what are called the "Three Cycles of Oral Lineage" of Chakrasamvara to three different disciples. The longest and most detailed Chakrasamvara practice was the Dagpo Nyengyu and was given to Gampopa. The middle length practice of Chakrasamvara called the Rechungpa Nyengyu was given to Rechungpa. And the shortest or condensed form, the Nagamdzong Nyengyu was given to Minzongrepa.

RECHUNGPA AND THE EIGHT WORLDLY DHARMAS

Rechungpa was regarded as very special by other dharma students because he had been to India three times and had received many special instructions. He was treated with great respect but Milarepa said to Rechungpa that he was becoming involved with the *eight worldly dharmas* because of this fame.[23] When one is respected by others, one has to receive that respect in an appropriate way which means not developing pride. It is like if you always get very elegant food, you could enjoy this, but you have to be very careful not to become attached to this food and develop these eight worldly dharmas.

Milarepa said, "If external sensory pleasures are a benefit to one's practice, then they are good. But if they increase the worldly dharmas, they are bad." Milarepa continued, "Marpa instructed me to avoid the eight worldly dharmas and to practice without external sensory pleasures. So I have practiced without external pleasures and I have been able to develop a few good qualities." Then he told Rechungpa that if he could practice without being involved with the eight worldly dharmas his practice would go well.

One night Rechungpa had a dream in which he saw Tibupa dancing dressed in bone jewelry. He gave him some meditation instructions. When Rechungpa woke up he thought, "I really must go back to India and see Tibupa again." And so he went to Milarepa and told him about this dream and he said, "I must really go to India again so please give me permission to go." But Milarepa replied, "There's no reason why you have to go to India. It's much better to stay here in Tibet. Tibet has been blessed by many great scholars and siddhas so you should just stay here in Tibet and practice. Dharma is something that you have to practice and internalize. You have to turn inward and practice. If you just keep running around and learning teachings on a verbal level, then your mind will go wild. You will start thinking that you are a very learned and great siddha. Your mind could become uncontrollable. It's much better to stay here and actually practice." So Rechungpa obeyed Milarepa and stayed in Tibet and kept on practicing instead of going back to India.

The pupils and Nyamas treated Rechungpa as being more important than Milarepa because he'd been to India so many times. Milarepa and Rechungpa had separate caves. One day a lot of people came to Rechungpa's cave and offered him a lot of very good food. Rechungpa thought, "Well, they've given me all this so they must have given even more to Milarepa. I wonder how much he's gotten?" So he went to see Milarepa and said, "Well the sponsors and patrons have come and they've given all this food so maybe we should hold a sacred feast (Skt. *ganachakra)* celebration for everyone." Milarepa said, "Yes, that would be a good idea."

Milarepa kept his food in a stone box and Milarepa said, "My food is in there." So Rechungpa went to look and he saw that it was all really bad food. When Rechungpa saw this, he felt very unhappy and thought, "People are treating me better than Milarepa, but I don't have any of the qualities he has. So the best thing I can do is go away because I can't stay here as his attendant and be in opposition to him. It's better if I go off to central Tibet or someplace far away." So he told Milarepa, "I'm going to central Tibet, please give me permission to go."

Then Milarepa sang a song to him saying:

Sometimes I meditate while I sleep so I have the meditation instructions for transforming a state of stupor into clarity or *clear light*. No one else has these instructions, so it would be good for you to practice them.

Sometimes I meditate as I eat so I have the meditation instructions for seeing all food and drink as being a sacred feast. No one else has these instructions, so it would be very good for you to practice them.

Sometimes I meditate as I'm going somewhere and so I have meditation instructions to see all traveling as circum-ambulating. No one else has these instructions, so it would be good for you to practice them.

I have the meditation instructions I use while I work so that all behavior becomes the true nature of phenomena, the *dharmata.* No one else has these instructions, so it would be good for you to stay here and receive them from me and practice them.

But Rechungpa said, "No, I really must go to central Tibet. I want to circumambulate Lhasa and go see Samye temple. I want also to go see Lodrak where Marpa lived." So Milarepa said,

When you are meditating that the guru is the Buddha, what do you gain by circumambulating Lhasa? If you want to see something, you can see your own mind. If you can see your own mind, what good is it to go and see Samye temple?

In meditation you need to cut through both the doubts that you have and if you can not do that, then there is nothing gained by going to see where Marpa lived.

So it's much better that you stay here and meditate. You won't get any benefit out of going off to some far off place.

But Rechungpa insisted that he really must go to central Tibet and so finally Milarepa said, "If you are going to go, then you really must receive instructions from me and do a retreat for forty days first." So Milarepa gave him instructions and the empowerments of Vajravarahi. When this empowerment was given, Rechungpa experienced Chakrasamvara actually appearing and holding the vase and giving the empowerment. Rechungpa was given the empowerments for the Vajravarahi practice with fifteen deities and the practice with seven deities, the practice with the five deities and the practice with a single deity. He received all these empowerments and practiced them. Then it was decided that he would go to central Tibet.

MILAREPA'S PROPHECY

Milarepa said, "So you've received these teachings and you should keep them and maintain them. Ideally you should not go to central Tibet now because the time has not come for you to go yet. It's better that you stay, but if you are going to insist on going, before you go you should circumambulate your cave where you practice and do one hundred prostrations and mandala offerings." But Rechungpa was so overjoyed to receive permission to go that he forgot to do the circumambulations, the prostrations, and the mandala offerings.

Milarepa warned Rechungpa, "When you go to central Tibet you will be bitten on the leg by a female dog." Milarepa also told him that there was a Nepalese master called Asu who had Eight Mahamudra Instructions and Milarepa gave him permission to receive instructions from Asu. Milarepa said, "It would be good to go and receive these instructions from him. They should be the same ones I received so it would be good to receive and practice them."

Finally Milarepa went to see Rechungpa off. He sat on a rock and thought Rechungpa would look back at him. But Rechungpa didn't. He just walked straight ahead without looking back at Milarepa. So Milarepa thought, "He doesn't have much faith since he hasn't turned around to look back at me." Consequently Milarepa created seven robbers at a location where Rechungpa hadn't arrived yet. When Rechungpa did arrive these seven robbers appeared and said, "We're going to beat you, rob you, and kill you!" Seeing these seven robbers, Rechungpa suddenly remembered Milarepa had told him to circumambulate his cave and do a hundred prostrations and mandala offerings and that he had forgotten to do so. He thought, "So now this obstacle is occurring!" He closed his eyes and meditated on Milarepa being on top of his head and he prayed to him. Then it seemed to become very quiet and when he opened his eyes, instead of seven robbers he saw seven yogis. These yogis said to him, "Who are you? Where do you come from? Who is your teacher? What do you practice?" Rechungpa thought, "These are no ordinary yogis. They must be emanations of my teacher." So he replied that his teacher was Milarepa and he was going to central Tibet and he practiced the instructions on the subtle channels and subtle winds.[24] At that point Milarepa himself appeared directly to him and said he was a good pupil with perfect *samaya* and unchanging faith in the teacher. He wished him farewell on his journey to central Tibet and gave him further instructions. This is the end of the eighth chapter which describes how Rechungpa received many meditation instructions from Milarepa and then left for central Tibet.

Naropa

Naropa was a famous scholar at Nalanda University in India when an ugly dakini visited him. She asked him if he understood the words or the meaning of the Buddhist teaching. When Naropa said he understood the words she jumped with joy, but when he said he understood the meaning, she wept. She told him he did not understand the meaning, so he must go study under "her brother" Tilopa. So Naropa set out on a long journey to find Tilopa and became his disciple.

A photograph taken before the cultural revolution of Rechungpa's Monastery. Above this monastery are caves in which Rechungpa meditated.

Chapter 5

Rechungpa Gathers Students

An old lady asked Rechungpa about the dharma. So Rechungpa sang a song to her about the nature of the mind. He said:

The nature of the mind is emptiness, like space, but in actual fact, space cannot really be used as an example for the mind because there's no awareness in space. Space is just empty and the mind also possesses awareness. So it's not just emptiness, it's clarity.

To explain the clarity of the mind, one could use an example of the sun and the moon. But actually this is not a good example because the sun and the moon are solid objects, whereas the mind is not. Also the sun and the moon change whereas the mind is completely stable and unchanging.

So one could say that the mind is stable and unchanging like a mountain. But, in fact, the mind is not like a mountain because a mountain is just an assembly of stones and earth whereas the mind is not made of matter. So the mind is empty and clear and stable and unchanging.

Then Rechungpa said it would be good if she could meditate and practice with these facts in mind. Feeling faith in Rechungpa, she asked him to come to her home. In her home was her old husband who also felt faith in Rechungpa and asked him to create a dharma connection.[25] Rechungpa sang the husband a song in which he explained he lived in caves, that his food and clothing were very poor, just whatever he could get hold of, and that he was traveling on pilgrimages

37

and practicing the different instructions he had received from his teacher.

They told Rechungpa they had no son, but they were very wealthy and asked if he could stay with them as their son and teacher. They offered him a very large and special turquoise. But Rechungpa said there was no point in staying with them for a long time because they wouldn't see any of his inner qualities but only become aware of his external faults. So Rechungpa prepared to leave. The word got around that a great lama was there and a lot of people gathered together and requested him to give them dharma teachings.

Rechungpa sang a song about the dharma which was very easy for everyone to understand.

In paradise in the god realms[26] when the harvest is planted, it immediately ripens so beings in this realm have no difficulty finding food. This wasn't because the gods in the god realm were skilled farmers, but because they had accumulated positive karma in their previous lives. They accumulated this positive karma by giving to others. It is very important therefore to apply oneself to the accumulation of merit.

In the hell realms, if one is stabbed by a sword and killed, one immediately comes alive again. This isn't because there are skilled physicians in the hell realm, but the effect of the negative karma that beings in this realm have accumulated. Therefore, it is important to be able to meditate on patience and avoid anger and negative actions.

As soon as beings in the hungry ghost realm eat food, they become hungry again. This isn't because they have large stomachs, but because they have accumulated negative karma in their past lives based on their greed and miserliness. As a result their hunger can't be satisfied.

We now have the opportunity to listen to dharma teachings and practice them. This is the result of our having come in contact with the dharma in previous lifetimes. So in this lifetime, we should use this opportunity to practice the dharma.

A Spiritual Song for a Lama's Wife

Having given teachings and advice Rechungpa left and went to an area called Turlung near Lhasa which is near the Tsurpu area.[27] When he arrived, he found a lama building a house. Rechungpa went to stay nearby and meditated there. The lama's wife saw him and went up to see him. Rechungpa asked for a noon meal. She thought, "Oh well, if I'm going to give him food, then he must do something for it." So she gave him some sewing to do and waited. Rechungpa didn't do any of the sewing. He just sat and meditated. She came back later and asked, "Well, have you done the sewing?" He replied, "No, I haven't done any sewing." She became angry and said, "You are asking, 'Give me food' and you haven't done any work, and therefore you are not worthy of being given food." So Rechungpa sang her a song in which he said:

> The snow lion is sometimes busy and sometimes not. He's busy because he's wandering around the snow mountains and he is not busy because he doesn't have any work to do. When he's going around the snow mountains, he has to be very careful and wary of blizzards.
>
> The tiger in the jungle is sometimes busy and sometimes not. He is busy because he is leaping around in the jungle. He is not busy in that he doesn't have work to do. But he has to be very careful and wary of hunters.
>
> I, Rechung Dorje Drak, am sometimes busy and sometimes not. I'm busy wandering from place to place and I'm not busy because I don't have any work to do. But I have to be very careful and wary of the Lord of Death.
>
> You are like a miserly person, but you don't have to waste your precious human existence. Life is not very long, and so you should use that time well. Giving me some food would be very beneficial for you.

After he sang this song, she felt faith in him and burst into tears and asked him to come into her home saying, "I must repent and confess that I scolded you." He told her that she should meditate on death and impermanence. She asked him to give her his blessing so that she wouldn't waste her human life and would be aware of death and impermanence and so practice dharma. Rechungpa went to her house to have lunch. The people working there said, "Well, we are all working and this man doesn't help us at all but just sits there with his back turned to us all the time. But as soon as it's lunch time, he's here straight away." The woman said, "You mustn't talk like that. This is a very special lama, a great siddha, and we should respect him and receive dharma teachings from him." So Rechungpa gave them teachings and they all felt trust in him and received these teachings and began dharma practice.

They asked him to go and live in the upper end of the valley where there was a cave that Padmasambhava had stayed in and which had therefore been blessed by him. Rechungpa said he wouldn't live there, but to form a connection with the blessing of Padmasambhava, he stayed there for one week.

RECHUNGPA RECEIVES A GIFT FOR MILAREPA

Rechungpa next traveled north to where he thought the Nepalese guru Asu would be. But the guru had already gone to Lhasa. However, there was a woman who was very ill and asked for his blessing. Through examining his own breath and his own subtle wind, Rechungpa realized that he would be able to cure this woman. He gave her a blessing and she was cured. Her family wanted to give him a lot of gifts for what he had done, but he wouldn't take anything except some dried meat. He took this dried meat, ground it up by beating it with a rock and put it in a cotton bag. They asked him what he was doing and he replied, "My guru Milarepa always eats just vegetables and if I put some of this meat in his food, it would be good for his health." When they heard that, one person thought, "Well, I must give you a lot more dried meat" and said, "I will make this offering to your teacher." So he was given a lot more dried yak meat that was ground up and put in cotton bags.

40

At this time Milarepa was in meditation in a cave at Nyantang. Because of his vast awareness, he knew of what was happening and said, "Today, Rechungpa has a very big present for me and he will arrive in three days time." After three days, Rechungpa arrived with the ground meat and they held a sacred offering feast. Milarepa was very happy and for a while Rechungpa stayed with him. All the other pupils and Nyamas who practiced on the lunar days said that Rechungpa should stay with Milarepa all the time. But Rechungpa said, "When I'm not with my teacher, then the desire to be with him always arises in my mind. So really I need to stay with him. If I do stay continually though, then an obstacle (of them worshiping me instead of him) will arise for his pupils and these Nyamas. So I have to go." Therefore Milarepa didn't ask Rechungpa to stay and after a while, Rechungpa left for central Tibet.

Rechungpa said he was going to leave and travel around the country in distant places. Milarepa escorted him part of the way and he said to him that he could study under teachers, receive their teachings, and if they were profound instructions, then he should practice them. But if they were not, then Rechungpa should just forget them. He said that he should go to the Yarlung valley where there was a very beautiful mountain that looks like rice leaves. If he were to stay and live there, it would be beneficial to many beings. However, he warned of a danger of Rechungpa being bitten by a worldly female dog. If that happened, he should pray to Milarepa.

RECHUNGPA MEETS A MONK

Rechungpa then traveled north and met a gathering of people accompanied by a very fine, well-dressed monk. When this monk met Rechungpa, he said, "You are a very good yogi, but it's a shame that you go around in such tattered clothing. It would be better if you became a monk." Rechungpa in reply sang him a song in which he said that the monk was very kind to express his compassion towards him, but he was a yogi and pupil of Milarepa, so he just spent his time meditating. If he were to become a monk, it would be only a superficial image. So it was much better that he stay just as he was, dressing in whatever he had, and doing his meditation.

41

Now this monk claimed that he himself had good conduct and had received many teachings and contemplated them. He had studied all these words of the teachings, but because meeting Rechungpa was a very great experience, he wanted Rechungpa to give him instructions. Rechungpa then explained that to practice the dharma, we first need to find a good teacher. When we have found a good teacher, the next thing to do is to receive all of the teachings from that lama. After having received these teachings, we should then practice them properly. If we can do all these three things, we can achieve Buddhahood in one lifetime. Following these instructions, this monk became a very good dharma practitioner, a great meditator, and siddha.

RECHUNGPA MEETS HIS MAIN DISCIPLE

One day Rechungpa arrived at a guest house and seeing everyone inside all involved with their own problems and work, he felt compassion for these people. However, there was one young man who came to Rechungpa and said he had come from a place where there was a cave blessed by Padmasambhava. This blessing made it a very good place to meditate. He said that he actually wanted to go and meet the famous Milarepa and his pupil Rechungpa. Looking at Rechungpa he said, "You look like someone who is a pupil of Milarepa so you must know Milarepa well." Rechungpa replied, "Milarepa and his pupils are at Nyantang and he is in good health." He then sang a spiritual song to all the people in this guesthouse saying that if they didn't use their precious human birth, it would be a great loss. He told them the mind is like a jewel, and if the mind is allowed to fall into samsara, that would be a great waste. The teachings of the guru are like *healing nectar* (Skt. *amrita)* and if we are lazy and don't practice, then that also is a great waste. Furthermore, our body is like an image of the Buddha, and if we just waste it, then that also is a great loss. So what we need to do is to use our life to practice the dharma rather than waste it.

A little while after he finished the song, a pupil of Milarepa's arrived at this guesthouse and seeing Rechungpa, he prostrated to him, saying "I am very fortunate today to have met Rechungpa." The young man who had been talking to him heard this and realizing he had actually been talking to Rechungpa burst into tears saying, "Do you have no compassion for me? You knew I was talking to you and you didn't tell me that you were Rechungpa. From now on I am going to follow you wherever you go. I'll be right behind you." Rechungpa said, "It's not that I had no compassion for you. I didn't say I was Rechungpa because I'm going to be wandering around from place to place. So there's no point in following me. It is much better that you go and meet Milarepa because he resides in one place and gives teachings to many pupils. Better go there and receive his teachings."

But this young man insisted on following Rechungpa and he became Rechungpa's main disciple, Rinchen Drak. So after that Rechungpa and Rinchen Drak traveled together. They went to Lhasa where they met the Nepalese guru Lama Pakpo and asked for teachings from him. He taught them the sacred dohas of Saraha and the Mahamudra instructions. Then in accordance with Milarepa's prophecy, they went to Yarlung Valley.

Before they left Lhasa, Lama Pakpo told them, "These Mahamudra instructions are very special and very important. You should practice them well. Tibetans are always receiving teachings from very high teachers, but no one else has these Mahamudra instructions except me. So you should take them and practice them carefully."

Marpa, The Translator

Marpa was the first person of the Kagyu lineage to be born in Tibet. He learned many languages and took three very dangerous trips to India to bring the Buddhist teachings to Tibet. These teachings were all but lost in India due to the Moslem invasion and a general decline of Buddhism in the land of its origin. Marpa's main disciple was Milarepa.

Chapter 6

Rechungpa and Latchi

When they arrived at the Yarlung valley, they went to the local ruler's house and began banging on the door. His daughter, Latchi, was furious at the yogis' knocking because her father was ill. She came to the door saying, "You yogis come around begging in the summer, you come around begging in the winter, you come around begging all the time." But when she opened the door and saw Rechungpa who was so handsome, her anger vanished. She said, "Oh, who are you and where did you come from?" He said, "My name is Rechung Dorje Drak and I'm a pupil of Milarepa" and told her all about himself. She then invited them in and went to tell her father about their arrival.

She said, "Someone called Rechung Dorje Drak has arrived and he is someone very special. I think if you see him it would be good for your illness." Her father replied, "Yes, this is very good because I had this auspicious dream and I'm sure that if he comes in that he'll be able to help me." So Rechungpa entered and blessed the father who got better. The father said to Rechungpa, "In Yarlung there are two very famous teachers, Milarepa and Rechungpa. Which of them are you a pupil of?" Rechungpa replied, "Well, I am a pupil of Milarepa and my name is Rechungpa." The father was very surprised and told him how fortunate he felt to receive a blessing from him.

Soon after Rechungpa's blessing had cured the local ruler of Yarlung, the ruler offered Rechungpa his palace and his high-spirited daughter Latchi. Previously, Milarepa had prophesied that if Rechungpa established a spiritual center on the side of the Yarlung Valley,[28] great benefit would arise for beings in the future. He also predicted that his leg would be bitten by a female dog. Both of these prophecies were about to be fulfilled.

Rechungpa lived at the king's palace in the Yarlung Valley, took Latchi as his consort and wife,[29] and stayed at the king's palace and became very famous. Everyone said, "This is a very impressive lama!" Many people came to see him and gave him many offerings. Then with his pupil Rinchen Drak he went to see the Nepalese master Asu to receive Mahamudra teachings. Asu gave Rechungpa and his pupil very detailed teachings called the "white instructions," the "red instructions," and the "black instructions" of Mahamudra. He gave instructions from sunrise to sunset and on through the night. The explanations and commentaries were long and detailed. Rechungpa found it very difficult to actually put these instructions into practice. He also found the actual meditation quite awkward and difficult. After receiving these instructions, Rechungpa sang a song to master Asu:

> In the beginning, I was able to develop the correct view. Then I was able to practice meditation perfectly. Then I was able to develop correct conduct and confidence in my true nature. All of this was due to the kindness of Milarepa.
>
> But now my view has become faulty; dullness and agitation have arisen in my meditation and the *eight worldly dharmas* have merged into my conduct.
>
> But you, the Nepalese master Asu, have the key for opening the door to the treasury of the instructions of Saraha and Maitripa. So please open this door and give me their Mahamudra instructions.

The master Asu upon hearing this was very unhappy and said he was going to enter retreat for fifteen days and that Rechungpa should also stay in retreat for that length of time.

The attendants to Rechungpa asked him, "Who is this Master Asu that you are studying under?" Rechungpa replied that in the past there was a great scholar with many pupils in Nepal. He also had a son, an ordinary person, and this was Asu. When Asu's father died, he was a businessman traveling between India and Nepal, but was not a dharma practitioner.

In the process of doing business, Asu learned Tibetan and came to know some translators. He then went to India and received teachings including the Mahamudra teachings of Saraha and others. He asked his own guru when he should begin teaching. His guru told him to wait fifteen years before teaching in Tibet because his Tibetan was not good enough. However, Asu did not follow his guru's direction and began teaching after twelve years.

When the master Asu came out of his retreat, he again gave the Mahamudra teachings on the view, the essence, and so on. But Rechungpa found that he hadn't really developed any realization that was any greater than he had gained from the teachings of Milarepa. So he and Rinchen Drak made a mandala offering to Asu and left for Lhasa.

RECHUNGPA TEACHES RIGHT VIEW IN LHASA

In Lhasa so many people came to receive teachings from Rechungpa that the monks living in Lhasa became very jealous of him. They said, "He doesn't keep any monastic vows like we do, so there really isn't any point for people to receive teachings from him. He shouldn't be teaching them!" Rechungpa replied to them, "This is how people without vows go walking" and he began walking on the water, just like he was walking on land. Then he said, "I just sleep in a state of complete stupor and this is how I go in and out of the house." He simply walked through the walls of the house. After performing these miracles, the monks developed great faith in him. They received teachings from him and did retreats and were able to develop realization.

Rechungpa then went to practice in sacred places that had the power of blessing. A few yogis also came to join him and said that they liked the unrestricted yogi's life where they could eat what they liked and do what they pleased. Rechungpa then said, "Yes, a yogi's life is a happy one, but the yogi also has to practice the dharma. If one becomes distracted from practice, then being a yogi is pointless. So one has to practice very carefully to keep one's vows. If one takes it too lightly, one will find out that a yogi's life in the end is not really an easy life."

47

He then sang them a song in which he said that contemplating death and impermanence is not enough because one needs also to practice the dharma. One might think that avoiding the *ten negative actions* and being aware of the faults of samsara is enough. But it isn't enough because one has to follow the very finest details of karma, of karma's actions, and karma's results. One might think that meeting a great teacher and receiving instructions is enough. But it isn't enough because one has to practice the teachings until one has gained realization and experience. One might think gaining stability of mind in meditation is enough. But it isn't because one needs to attain something that is more difficult than that which is realization of the nature of mind.

RECHUNGPA TEACHES MARPA'S STUDENTS

Then Rechungpa went to southern Tibet to visit the cave where Marpa had stayed and practiced. When he was there, he met Ngok Shedang Dorje who was the son of Ngok Choku Dorje, one of the main pupils of Marpa. Shedang Dorje was a good practitioner and when he found out that Rechungpa was there, he came to ask for teachings from him. When they met, Rechungpa began to praise Tibupa saying that he'd been to India and had met Tibupa. He described how wonderful Tibupa was and described the qualities he had. Rechungpa praised Tibupa a lot and Shedang Dorje thought, "Actually he owes a lot more to Milarepa than he does to Tibupa. He hasn't said a thing about Milarepa and just goes on about Tibupa. He can't be really very good" and decided not to receive any teachings from Rechungpa.

So then Rechungpa went to see Tsurton Wange Dorje, one of the four main pupils of Marpa still living. Rechungpa went to see him because he thought Tsurton Wange had the very profound teachings of Guhyasamaja. When they met, Tsurton Wange asked him who he was and was pleased to hear that he was a pupil of Milarepa. Tsurton Wange said, "My teacher was Marpa and Marpa went three times to India where he received teachings from Naropa and Maitripa. In particular, Marpa passed on to me the teachings of the father tantra Guhyasamaja. With these instructions one is able to grasp the subtle winds (Tib. *lung)* with one's hand and I can give you these instructions."

Rechungpa thought, "Well, this teaching is very profound so I must receive it." Then Tsurton Wange taught him the five stages of the Guhyasamaja teachings. When Rechungpa had finally received them all, he thought they were not really all that profound. Tsurton Wange said, "I taught all the teachings on the grasping of the subtle winds and how to hold on to the subtle winds." But Rechungpa replied, "Is that it?" Tsurton Wange replied, "I'm old now, but I will practice a few days and then show you some more things." After a few more days Tsurton Wange showed Rechungpa various techniques for controlling the subtle winds, but Rechungpa was not impressed. He thought, "These teachings are not very much. I have learned much more from Milarepa." So he told Tsurton Wange he had received much better teachings than these from his own teacher, Milarepa. Tsurton Wange then asked, "What kind of experience have you had then?" Rechungpa sitting in the vajra (full lotus) posture with the help of his subtle winds then rose six feet up into the air and sang a song saying, "I'm Rechungpa and I've had a great deal of experience! I'm a student of Milarepa. I've been able to understand the nature of the ordinary mind consciousness." Then Rechungpa held the *vayu* of earth and he sank down into the earth up to his waist and in that position he sang another song. He sang, "I am a pupil of Milarepa and his teachings on control of the vayus is much greater than this. He can fly in the sky, he can walk on water, he can pass through the earth. He can ride on a rock as if it were a horse! So Milarepa is not just skilled in talking. He has the actual powers developed through his practice."

Tsurton Wange was very surprised by this and thought, "This is so good!" He then said, "In my teachings the actual explanation is very important. As a result of that I can give very good explanations, but in terms of practice I don't have the power for miraculous abilities or control the subtle winds. Whereas you, Rechungpa, being a pupil of Milarepa, teaching is not the main point but practice is the most important thing. Now you have been able to gain this kind of achievement."

So Rechungpa stayed with Tsurton Wange and his monks and

taught them the *tummo* instructions on producing heat in the depths of winter. They would sit and practice in the cold of winter in just cotton robes.

Then Rechungpa returned to Yarlung and stayed with Latchi at the king's palace there. The king said, "I've met a very special teacher who gave me instructions and I'm practicing them. I'm wealthy and have everything that I need. There's no one happier than I." So Rechungpa thought, "The king is becoming very proud and this is not good for him!"

He therefore sang him a song saying that the *chakravartin*, the universal ruler, has seven precious possessions but these seven possessions are not permanent.

Instead of the precious wheel, one needs the precious wheel of faith. If one has this faith then one will be able to be diligent and apply oneself to the practice of good actions.

Instead of a precious jewel, one needs the precious jewel of wisdom. If one has that, then one will be able to accomplish whatever oneself or others need.

Instead of the precious queen, one needs the precious queen of conduct.

Instead of the precious minister one needs the precious minister of conscience because with that one will avoid doing wrong actions.

Instead of the precious elephant, one needs the precious elephant of meditative stability because with that one will be able to gather the accumulations of merit and wisdom.

Instead of the precious horse, one needs the precious horse of diligence because it will be able to carry one to a place where there are no more mind poisons.

Instead of the precious general, one needs the precious general of hearing the correct teachings because if one has received the correct teachings one will eliminate all incorrect views.

So these are the kind of royal possessions one needs.

Having said that Rechungpa was able to diminish the pride of the king.

RECHUNGPA AND THE TURQUOISE

Then the king of Yarlung said, "If you are going to stay I am going to build you a monastery." So a monastery was built called Rechungpuk which was the residence for Rechungpa and the many students who came there to receive teachings. In particular, there was one destitute person who used to come often. He'd come in the morning and no one knew where he came from and in the evening he would leave and no one would know where he went. He kept coming, saying, "Please help me. Please help me." and requested Rechungpa's help. Eventually, Rechungpa said to him, "Well, what do you want?" and he replied, "What I want is for you to give me wealth and possessions so I won't be poor any more." Rechungpa replied, "You can always stay here with me and if you think of something you need, just tell me and I will give it to you."

In the valley there was also an old couple. One day the old man talked to his wife about a very special turquoise stone that they had saying, "We are quite wealthy and if we just keep this turquoise hidden it is not going to be of any use to anyone. If it's displayed, people will quarrel and fight over it and it won't do any good either. We, however, have this very special teacher Rechungpa so wouldn't it be good to give it to him?" The wife said, "Well, that is what I've been thinking all along but I didn't want to say it." So they agreed to give this turquoise to Rechungpa and invited Rechungpa and many other people over for a nice meal. They gave a lot of offerings to Rechungpa and then, very secretly so no one would see, they gave him the turquoise. But the king's daughter Latchi got a glimpse of this turquoise while it was being given.

Then this beggar came along who kept saying, "Give me this." When no one was looking, Rechungpa gave him the turquoise and said to him, "I think you had better leave now. I don't think you should stay around here because if anybody or my pupils see you with it, it will be taken from you. So you'd better go away!" Without anyone knowing the beggar left with the turquoise.

But Latchi was quite sure Rechungpa was going to give it to her and kept waiting for this to happen. But, of course, Rechungpa didn't give her the turquoise. When Latchi didn't get the turquoise from him, she thought, "Well, Rechungpa isn't wearing this turquoise so I must be the one who gets it." She tried all sorts of methods to get the turquoise, but none of them seemed to work. One day when Rechungpa was away she thought, "Well, I must go in and have a look and see what this turquoise is really like." She entered his room and started looking for the turquoise but, of course, the turquoise wasn't there. But there was another turquoise that someone else had given him a long time before. When she saw this turquoise, she was very pleased with it and stayed in the room sometimes putting it around her neck to see how it looked in the mirror. Sometimes she put it in her hair and on her ears to see what it looked like. After a while she thought, "I mustn't let him find out that I've been here looking at this turquoise" and put it back exactly where she had found it and left the room pretending that she didn't know anything about the turquoise.

At a later time Rechungpa was out one day and some deformed beggars asked him, "Please give us something very valuable that is very easy to hide so we won't have it stolen from us; something very light so we can carry it easily; something which will give us a large amount when we sell it." Rechungpa felt compassion for these beggars and thought, "What can I give them? Oh! I have that piece of turquoise. I'll give them that." So he said to them, "Go around to the back of the king's palace with me" and then went to his room, got the turquoise, mixed some *tsampa* (barley dough) and put the turquoise in the middle of it. Then he threw it out the back window to the beggars saying, "Here! Take this tsampa but don't eat it here. Take it a long way away and eat it there." Some of the beggars thought, "We've come here asking this great lama for something valuable and all he's given us is a lump of tsampa. Not only that but he's asked us to go off somewhere else and eat it! We might just as well eat it here

52

right now." But one of the beggars said, "No. Rechungpa is a really great lama so he must have some special reason for asking us to eat it somewhere else." The beggars nevertheless started dividing the dough up among themselves and finding the turquoise made them all very happy. The beggars went to the north and sold the turquoise for a lot of money and settled there. This place become known as Trangde in Tibetan which means "poor man's place." Although they had become wealthy from selling this turquoise, by the time they arrived at this place they were quite destitute again. So that is how Trangde become known as "poor man's village."

A temple near Yarlung was completed and it was going to be consecrated so everyone was going to the consecration dressed in their best jewelry and finery. Princess Latchi thought, "Tomorrow I will go to the consecration dressed in my best clothes and riding my finest horse. I'll bring all my servants and I'll have Rechungpa come with me because he is so handsome. Also I'll have those two turquoise stones because I know he has the one the old couple gave him and the other one I found in his room." She said to Rechungpa, "Well, tomorrow we'll go to the consecration and I thought we'd go on very beautiful horses and I know you have two turquoise pieces. So perhaps you can lend them to me so I can wear them as my jewelry." Rechungpa replied that he'd given them both away to beggars. At this she became very angry, her face darkened, and she walked out of the room. Rechungpa thought, "This is very samsaric. Her mind has become very involved with these pieces of turquoise. It is a good thing that I gave them away to the beggars because no good would have come to her being so attached to these turquoise pieces!" Meanwhile the princess was thinking, "He's given those two turquoise stones away to the beggars after we have given him all these nice clothes, fine food, a house, everything. When it comes to beggars, he's the beggar!"

Usually the princess brought Rechungpa very fine food, but after this she sent a servant with some very ordinary food. But Rechungpa was busy meditating and therefore didn't bother to eat. When she found out he hadn't eaten, she brought him some really awful food on an ugly plate, the sort of food one would give a beggar. Then she said giving it to him, "If you can't eat the other food, then being a beggar, you can eat this kind of food."

When Latchi gave him this food, Rechungpa thought, "Oh, this is very auspicious" and carried on meditating. When she came back and saw he hadn't eaten, she went and got a stick and began hitting him. Rechungpa thought, "Oh, this is very good." Rechungpa then took off all the fine clothes that he had been wearing and put on his cotton clothes, got his walking stick, and began to leave.

When Latchi saw that he was going, she thought, "Oh no! I have made a mistake and for this he is walking out on me. He's very attached to his books so I'll hide them and then he won't leave." So she did this but Rechungpa said, "I don't care if you hide my books. I'm going." As he began to leave, Latchi took hold of his clothes and begged him not to go. Rechungpa said, "I've made a big mistake. I left the mountains and came to live in a town. I left my lama and went to live with a king. I took off my cotton clothes and started wearing the clothes of a wealthy person. I left my dharma brothers and sisters and went to live with ministers and important officials. I'm not going to continue making this mistake."

Using his miraculous abilities, Rechungpa held his subtle winds and moved off at great speed down the Yarlung Valley to where the Yarlung River meets the Zangpo, the main river running through Tibet that becomes the Brahmaputra. When he arrived there, he found boats and ferrymen for crossing the river. "Take me across the river," he said. The ferryman said, "You're a strange person! When does a person get a boat for himself for crossing the river? You will have to wait here until other passengers have come." Rechungpa thought that he couldn't wait so he took off his cotton robe and laid it down on the water and using his stick as an oar rowed across to the other side of the river. On seeing this, the ferryman felt great faith in Rechungpa and rowed to him and said, "Please forgive me for not taking you across in the boat. Please give me meditation instructions." So Rechungpa gave him meditation instructions and the ferryman later became a yogi.

Rechungpa then headed west through Tibet. Someone offered

him some dried meat. He took it, ground it up to powder and put it in a cotton bag to take to Milarepa. At that time Milarepa was in a cave giving dharma teachings to his pupils and said, "Oh, Rechungpa is coming and he is bringing a present and the whole valley will not be big enough for it. He'll be here in two days time." When Rechungpa arrived, the other pupils said, "Milarepa said you were coming with a present and the valley wouldn't be big enough for it. What have you brought? Rechungpa replied, "I have brought this bag of powdered meat." They made a soup out of it and Milarepa ate it and said, "Ah, the valley of my stomach isn't big enough to contain this present!" Then Milarepa added, "Tomorrow I am going to give the empowerment of Chakrasamvara with sixty-two deities. So everyone has to give a mandala offering except Rechungpa who doesn't have to give anything." Rechungpa wondered why he wasn't required to give an offering, but the next day when he came to the empowerment, he saw that in the mandala was the big turquoise that he had given the beggar.

When Rechungpa saw this turquoise, his skin began to tingle and he said, "What is that turquoise doing there?" Then he suddenly realized, "Samsara has no essence and there is no greater teacher than my teacher!"

Milarepa

Milarepa was Tibet's greatest saint. Out of revenge he killed many relatives using black magic in his early life. He then repented and became Marpa's disciple. In order to purify the negative karma he had created, Marpa put him through many arduous trials. Milarepa overcame these ordeals and received the teachings from Marpa. He then spent the rest of his life in retreats in caves in the high Himalayas. He passed the teachings on to Rechungpa and Gampopa who helped found what is now the Kagyu lineage.

Chapter 7

Milarepa's Final Teachings to Rechungpa

In the previous chapter Rechungpa experienced an obstacle but due to the compassion and blessing of Milarepa it was removed. Rechungpa came to see Milarepa and Milarepa gave him the Chakrasamvara empowerment of the sixty-two deities. After this Milarepa said that Rechungpa had very stable love and compassion and faith. But if it were not for Milarepa's own compassion and blessing, he would experience obstacles.

Then Milarepa sang a song to Rechungpa in which he explained how his miraculous powers and manifestations had been able to help Rechungpa. Rechungpa's great compassion and his ability to give without attachment allowed Milarepa to remove his obstacles. He said that he, Milarepa, had manifested as a beggar and had gone to see Rechungpa. Because of Rechungpa's compassion he had received this turquoise and had taken it as an offering for the future Chakrasamvara empowerment. He said that one's happiness depends on other beings because if one helps others, then this creates the causal conditions for one's own happiness. If one, however, harms others, this will just create bad karma. Therefore one should approach the mandala of the sixty-two deities of Chakrasamvara and confess whatever bad actions one has done and make a commitment not to repeat them again in the future.

At first Rechungpa was not able to say anything because he was so amazed. But eventually he felt the confidence to say something. First he confessed the actions of body: that he felt a great desire for physical comforts and that he had been very distracted by material possessions. In terms of speech, he confessed that he had said many things that may not have been true. He confessed also that he had a great attachment to good food and to meat and to alcohol. He said, "I make this confession to my guru's speech." As for his mind, he said he wished to be happy all the time. Because he always wanted to be happy, he gave rise to the disturbing emotions. He also wanted to be famous and because of this desire he had engaged in a lot of incorrect conduct. He also wanted to be an important person and therefore performed many wrong actions. All these things he confessed to his teacher.

Milarepa was very pleased with Rechungpa's confession but the yogi Shiwao said, "Rechungpa has complete control of the subtle winds (Skt. *prana*, Tib. *lung*) in his body and he has also great compassion for beings and has benefited them. Why does he have to make a confession?" Milarepa replied that in terms of sensory pleasures there is a certain degree that one could enjoy, but if one succumbs, then one becomes too involved in sensory pleasures so one has to be very careful. It's all a question of degree.

Then Milarepa gave instructions to Rechungpa and sang a song describing how his own realizations and experiences developed. He sang about how to eliminate obstacles and hindrances. This advice was a great benefit to Rechungpa and the other pupils.

MILAREPA INTERPRETS RECHUNGPA'S DREAMS

Rechungpa said he saw many signs and omens in his dreams and asked Milarepa about them. In one dream there was a dog and this dog was carrying a load of sheep wool on its back. It was also writing as it was going along and barking very loudly. Eighty-four people came to meet this dog. He asked Milarepa what the dream meant. Milarepa said, "The dog is like a friend and represents one's dharma companions and the wool shows a very soft and loving mind because wool is very soft. The writing indicates skill in words and terms. The barking loudly is the sign of being able to sing spiritual songs. The eighty-four people coming to meet this dog signify that you will live to be eighty-four years old."

In another dream Rechungpa took off his clothes and washed his body which then changed into a bird. He flew up to the top of a tree and on top of this tree was a mirror that he looked into. When he asked Milarepa what that meant, Milarepa said that taking off his clothes signified taking off the worldly life and washing his body was cleaning himself with the meditation instructions, that is, making himself stainless by using the meditation instructions. The bird's body was love and compassion. Of its two wings, one was the wing of the accumulation of merit and the other wing was the accumulation of wisdom. Flying to the top of the tree was flying to the top of the tree of bodhichitta, enlightened mind. The mirror was a sign given by the dakinis to show him what had happened.

Another dream was that he was riding a donkey but he was sitting on it backwards facing the tail. He was dressed in a *rewa*, which is a rough, black cloth made of yak hair. Because he was riding backwards and wearing such a rough cloth, Rechungpa thought this a very bad dream. But Milarepa said the donkey was a symbol of going on the path of the *Mahayana* and his being backwards on the donkey showed that he was turning his back to samsara and going towards nirvana. *Rewa* in Tibetan also means "hope" so Rechungpa's wearing this cloth meant that he would be a focus for the hopes of other beings.

Then Milarepa said to Rechungpa that he had now given him all of the meditation instructions so there was no reason for him to stay any longer and it would be better if he traveled from place to place. If he went from here to somewhere else it would be of very great benefit to beings. On hearing this Rechungpa said, "Have I really received all of the instructions? Are you sure that there are not any still left to be given?" Milarepa said, "The most profound instruction which I still have not given to you, I will give you when you leave. But everything else that I have received from Marpa I have given to you." Rechungpa was very happy to hear this and asked Milarepa, "Who is going to hold the lineage of your instructions and how long are you going to live? And what token is there of my having served you for so many years?"

Milarepa said that Marpa had many pupils, but of them all only he had been given the complete instructions. So to be sure these meditation instructions would not be wasted, Milarepa was spending the rest of his life practicing them. He also had many pupils: some who had achieved Buddhahood, some who had achieved the *bodhisattva level*, and some who had only created a connection with the dharma. From these, Gampopa would hold the lineage of the transmission of the special instructions given to him. It was prophesied by the dakinis that Rechungpa would be a principal pupil of Milarepa and have many pupils who would go directly to the Buddha-realms without leaving a physical body behind. Because Rechungpa himself was such a great practitioner, an emanation of Tilopa would come to be his pupil and Rechungpa should give him the orally transmitted instructions. But these orally transmitted instructions should not be given to people who didn't appreciate or have faith in the dharma.

Then Milarepa said to Rechungpa, "It would be very good if you went to very special and powerful places and practiced there. If you do that, it will be of very great benefit to beings in the future. You don't need to worry about me because I have complete power over the elements and when the time comes for my death, there will be no need to instruct me on what to do. Also *sacred relics* (Tib. *ringsels*) that will be left from my body will be taken by the dakinis to the pure realms. You don't need to worry about them either."

When Rechungpa thought about leaving, he thought, "There isn't really any point in my going off to these places. I should really stay here with my teacher." So he said to Milarepa, "I don't really want to go away. I want to stay here with you!" And Milarepa said, "When I tell you not to go, you go away. When I tell you to go, you won't! You shouldn't stay with me. You should go away because if you go to these other places, there will be a very great benefit for many beings from that action. So, you should visit these places."

Then Milarepa said now that he had given these meditation instructions to Rechungpa, he should maintain them, practice them and never forget them. And he added, "My emanations will come and spy on you sometimes so it's better that you go now. I've given you all these instructions but there is one remaining one that I won't give to you here but when we've gone some distance." So they walked a little while and Rechungpa was wondering what this instruction was. When they got to the appointed place Milarepa said, "Either you are going to die or death is going to come to you, so you have got to be very diligent." He lifted up his robe to show Rechungpa his bottom and because he had practiced so much sitting on the earth, all of the skin on his bottom had become very thick and hardened. And he said, "This is how you should practice. You need this kind of diligence." Then Milarepa said:

You should practice *tummo*, the inner heat practice, in order to develop realization. You should also wear only cotton clothing. For food you should eat only of meditation (of samadhi). If you can do this you will be free of many obstacles and be able to benefit beings.

You shouldn't stay in one place for too long. Keep moving from one place to another and forget all about the eight worldly dharmas. You should impart the instructions of the oral lineage to individuals with faith and not to someone who does not have faith in the dharma.

I am going to pass away on the full moon (the fifteenth day of the first Tibetan month) of the Rabbit year (1123 C.E.) so you should come back to see me. Until that year you don't need to come back to see me again. You go from place to place and you'll be able to work to benefit others.

Then Rechungpa left and as he was going he was able to see Milarepa in the distance. He recited supplications to him. Finally, he looked back from very far away and he could still see Milarepa and the others there in the distance and thought, "Oh no! I can't possibly leave! I have to go back!" Then he thought, "Well, it is my guru's command that I'll help a lot of beings, so I suppose I must do it." With a lot of diligence he forced himself to go on.

Now we will discuss the section on how he traversed the bodhisattva levels, how special realizations were born in his mind, and, in particular, how he tamed various disciples by means of special empowerments and oral instructions. Students were shown the paths and bodhisattva levels and where to spread the teachings. Milarepa gave a prophecy to Rechungpa saying, "At this point, you have perfected all the practices and have attained a supreme understanding, so now is the time for you to go to central Tibet. In the future we should have one more meeting, which will be in the year of the hare. You should come back and meet with me. But, before that time, you should stay in central Tibet."

Along the path to central Tibet Rechungpa met many disciples. In particular, he came upon several Varjayana practitioners performing a fire sadhana. One of the practitioners turned to Rechungpa and said, "This is how we do our fire sadhana. How do you yogins do it?" Rechungpa then sang a song to them saying:

For practice one has to tame the disturbing emotions. Your fire offering is the taming of external obstacles and demons.

For practice what must be burned are the inner disturbing emotions. Only burning these will bring about true benefit.

For practice one must have the inner wisdom blazing. Burning these outer substances will not bring about much benefit.

We yogins conduct our fire offering by resting in uncontrived natural mind. Within this we burn the fire of non-dual wisdom. What we burn up is our own discursive thoughts which is the wood of our inner clinging. With this our fire offering brings about the path to liberation.

Having heard this song, one of the Varjayana practitioners felt very great faith in Rechungpa and then received many oral instructions from him. After practicing all these teachings from Rechungpa, this disciple passed on the teachings to five hundred disciples. In this way, there was an unbroken dharma lineage starting from this disciple.

As Rechungpa continued to travel along the road, he came upon a scholar debating with several practitioners. Rechungpa said to them, "You don't need to debate among yourselves. I will resolve any doubts for you." He then sang a song for them:

> I am a very happy yogi.
> Having realized that samsaric confusion has no substance, I developed great renunciation and sadness, and applied myself to the practice of samadhi.
> Having practiced samadhi, I obtained the ultimate fruition, therefore I am very happy indeed.
> Because I constantly remember to supplicate my guru, I have received his blessings.
> In this way, no matter what I am practicing, there are no obstacles that arise in my practice and my own mind and my guru's mind have become inseparable. True meditative experience and realization have arisen in my mind. Therefore I have no need for bias against other dharma traditions.
> But I have the confidence that arises from understanding my own mind.

Having heard this song, the debaters felt great faith, stopped debating, and said, "What you have said is wonderful, so, please give us some advice about the best method for practice?"

Rechungpa then sang to them:

> It is very wonderful you have attained the precious human body endowed with the freedoms and resources. However, it is also extremely important to have a mind of faith.
> It is very good to understand clearly the oral instructions on death and impermanence. However, even more important is to attend your teacher and to have great devotion for him or her.

Receiving and understanding oral instructions is very good; however, it is even better to liberate your mind from the disturbing emotions.

Therefore, whatever practice you do, do not let your mind wander, but rest in an uncontrived, unfabricated state.

Always regard your physical body as the body of a deity. Always regard your speech as the mantra of the deity. Always regard your mind as inseparable bliss-emptiness.

In the same way, do not let your mind wander from the essential quality of samsara and nirvana. This is extremely important.

Having heard this teaching by Rechungpa, many students were able to perfect their understanding.

Previously, Milarepa had given a prophecy that, if Rechungpa went to the north, to Penul which is north of Lhasa, he would be able to bring about great benefit for many sentient beings. This was a place where many Kadampa teachers lived. So Rechungpa went to a particular monastery that was headed by a Kadampa spiritual teacher, named Miserwa. As soon as he arrived, Miserwa was rather condescending and said some rather negative things about Rechungpa. Rechungpa responded by singing a song to him. He sang:

All of you very learned ones here, please listen carefully to my song.

In my meditation inner realization has arisen in my mind; therefore, I have no fear of your criticisms. It seems to me that exactly what you need to do is to practice.

In my meditation, my body is engaged in inner heat practice. Therefore, I have no fear of cold and do not need any kind of beautiful body. So, again it seems to me that what you need is to practice.

You learned ones rely on the reading transmissions of the texts and studying the Buddhist Canon, whereas we yogins practice on developing our own inner experience. It seems to me you need to practice.

This gave the teacher Miserwa great faith. He said, "Previously I had heard of the many great qualities of Milarepa and Rechungpa, and now I am extremely pleased to finally meet you. Please teach me the dharma, so that we can have a dharmic connection."

Rechungpa then sang him a song in which he said:

What is my view? My view is to meditate and to realize directly the true nature of reality. I don't particularly care much for the studying of words and terms.

Then how should I meditate? I should meditate directly on the true nature of mind, free from any concept or imagination. I don't particularly care for developing all different kinds of concepts and thoughts.

What is my action? My action is based upon the signs of samadhi that has arisen within. I do not particularly care for good actions that are hypocritical.

Again Miserwa felt very great faith in Rechungpa, and received teachings on Mahamudra as well as teachings on the practice of Vajrapani.

Then Rechungpa met another teacher named Chinawa. Chinawa displayed several miracles to Rechungpa, but Rechungpa responded with greater miracles and so Chinawa developed great faith toward Rechungpa.

Later Rechungpa went to a monastery that was headed by a teacher named Urthurpa. He walked right in and sat right down among the monks who were sitting in a row. The teacher Urthurpa said, "Uh! This will not do, to have a goat come in the midst of sheep."

He then proceeded to throw Rechungpa out of the monastery. Rechungpa began a song:

I offer a song to all of you Kadampa monks. Please listen carefully. One must know that one's own body is the mandala of the deity. If one does not know this, then wearing yellow robes will not be of much benefit. It seems that wearing the robes of a monk develops pride so that you don't actually realize that your own body is extraordinary.

One must also know the true nature of speech. If one does not understand this, then one will not become enlightened by simply chanting. When you look at your speech, you feel great pride; however, you have not really understood that the true nature of speech is the subtle winds and the subtle channels.

One must also understand that the mind is of the nature of dharmakaya, enlightenment. If you don't understand this, you will not become enlightened by means of words. Based on your studying of the dharma, you have developed pride to the extent that your mind has simply become extremely ordinary.

Having heard this song by Rechungpa, the Kadampa teacher realized he was wrong so he sent two monks outside to invite Rechungpa inside. Rechungpa saw these two monks coming and thought, "Oh no, since I've criticized them by saying they don't have any realization, they're coming out to beat me. If they beat me, I'd better display some miracle in order to tame them and create benefit in the situation."

One of the khenpos (senior monks) however came out and said, "That was a wonderful song that you sang. Why don't you sing it again?" Rechungpa replied, "Well, I can't remember exactly what I sang. But I would be glad to sing you a new one."

Rechungpa then sang a song in which he said that he wasn't very happy about seeing the state of certain dharma practitioners who were following the activities of the eight worldly dharmas and therefore had not entered into the true path of dharma. So they should abandon these outward activities and rest thier mind in an uncontrived state. If they do not abandon the disturbing emotions, they will obtain neither relative nor absolute fruition. To abandon these disturbing emotions and the suffering they create, they must meditate.

Having heard this second song, the teachers and all the disciples felt great faith, and were then able to practice the correct path.

Gampopa

Gampopa was a physician who was unable to prevent his wife and children from dying in an epidemic. After this, he began a spiritual quest where he met a number of Kadampa teachers who taught him Buddhist philosophy and logic. He also studied with Milarepa who taught him the Six Yogas of Naropa and Maitripa's Mahamudra meditation. Gampopa was able to combine the Kadampa teachings with Milarepa's practice instructions and establish the first Kagyu Monasteries. Gampopa is also known for writing the *Jewel Ornament of Liberation* which outlines the complete Buddhist path.

Chapter 8

Rechungpa Visits Five Sacred Places

M ilarepa had prophesied that if Rechungpa went to central Tibet, he would benefit many beings and have many pupils doing practice. Following his guru's instructions Rechungpa went to central Tibet. He traveled from cave to cave practicing, meeting students, giving empowerments, and giving meditation instructions. He sang spiritual songs and gave dharma teachings to many people throughout central and northern Tibet.

1. YERBA

.

When Padmasambhava came to Tibet at the invitation of King Trisong Detsen in the seventh century, Samye Monastery was established. It became the main place for dharma teachings and for translating texts from Sanskrit into Tibetan. The main place for practice by Padmasambhava's students was a cave called Yerba, "moon cave" meaning a very special spiritual place. Eighty famous siddhas gained their accomplishments by practicing in retreat here. It had such powerful blessing that Rechungpa went there to meditate.

While Rechungpa was in Yerba, many pupils arrived to receive the Hevajra empowerment. When Rechungpa gave this empowerment, pupils had unusual experiences. Some had a vision of the Hevajra mandala and saw a rain of flowers. Others actually saw Rechungpa appearing as the Hevajra mandala. Still others heard celestial music accompanied by a rain of flowers. Everyone had a special experience from the Hevajra empowerment.

Eventually, Tsurton Wangye Dorje, one of Marpa's pupils came to see Rechungpa. He told Rechungpa that he had received the teachings on the tantras and held the transmissions and had passed them on to others, yet he felt his mind had become distracted. If he didn't get special meditation instructions from Rechungpa, he thought that he might face great difficulties in the *bardo* when he died. So Rechungpa taught him the instructions on Mahamudra and *Phowa* and the teachings on the bardo. Tsurton Wangye Dorje thus received great benefit from these teachings.

Rechungpa taught the bardo teachings, the instructions for the transition from this life to the next. These instructions on the bardo are very important. Through these instructions one is able to close the entrance to the six realms of samsara and thus attain Buddhahood in one lifetime. Rechungpa also explained that in between his stomach and back are the subtle channels that carry the subtle winds. With these instructions of using the subtle winds and channels Tsurton Wangye Dorje received great blessings.

Rechungpa had many special pupils such as Drogomrepa and Takshorepa who also received the instructions for these practices. These pupils practiced his instructions and passed them on to others, establishing Rechungpa's lineage. Rechungpa was asked to sing a song of rejoicing for their success. Rechungpa sang a spiritual song of joy:

How pleasant and happy it is to practice the dharma. But when I see other people involved in nondharmic activities, I feel that because this is occurring within us it is creating an error in the ways of people. So I make sure that I am practicing the dharma. Then, once again, I feel very happy.

Presently you are very happy practicing the dharma. Should you begin to lose interest in the dharma and become lost in worldly activities, you will later feel regret and unhappiness thinking, "I haven't been practicing the dharma so I must be careful to avoid that happening again!"

I have seen many dharma practitioners but I can also see that many have not entered onto the correct path. I, myself, received teaching from very special teachers and was able to follow a correct path and so I am very happy.

You must be very careful that your dharma practice is correct and that your dharma is not just talk. The dharma has to be practiced if it is going to be the true path.

I saw a great number of meditators who did not have good meditation teachers. When I saw that and knew that I had such a great meditation teacher as Milarepa, I felt very happy and very fortunate. It is important to develop devotion. But for this devotion to increase you should be careful that it isn't temporary or it will decline.

There are many teachers who make many false claims such as "Through this practice you will achieve Buddhahood." Then when you investigate, you find it is a false claim because there isn't any significant practice of the dharma involved. But when I think of myself I make no false claims or fall into false external pretexts. This makes me feel very happy. In the future avoid making exaggerated claims or presenting false teachings.

2. Chimpu

After having sung this song of advice, Rechungpa traveled with about fifteen of his pupils to Samye Monastery.[30] When they arrived, they met Takdor Yeshe who was in charge of Samye Monastery. He said, "You yogis! You don't have any real dharma practice because it's all superficial. You're really nothing at all! If you yogis are such great meditators I don't need to open the door for you. Through your miraculous abilities you can open the door and get in by yourselves, meet the deities, and do your prayers."

To correct this erroneous treatment, Rechungpa then performed a miracle. Using his cotton robe as wings he flew around Samye Monastery three times and finally landed on top of the temple. When he did that, all of the doors opened by themselves so that everyone could go in and see the sacred statues and thangkas there. Also when the doors opened the sound of music could be heard. Sometimes while Rechungpa was appearing in space, he became ten Rechungpa's going in different directions, singing songs, and sitting in the cross-legged posture. At one point he merged into space, completely disappearing and rainbows appeared and formed a tent over Samye Monastery. Then the rainbows gathered together and went in the direction of Chimpu. Everyone was filled with faith in Rechungpa and they all went off in the direction of the rainbows towards Chimpu which was some distance away. When they got to Chimpu, they found Rechungpa meditating under a tree.

Upon arriving there, people wanted to confess their negative deeds and for having criticized Rechungpa. They asked Rechungpa for dharma teachings. They received dharma teachings and the one who had criticized Rechungpa the most became one of his greatest pupils, Tagom Yeshe Dorje. People then asked Rechungpa to live there permanently and if he couldn't, at least to stay a few years. Rechungpa, however, could see that there weren't many pupils in that area and that there would be many more in other places, so he stayed just for twenty-one days. During that time he gave dharma teachings and gained disciples.

3. SANGRI

Rechungpa then travelled to Sangri which was the seat of the great female saint Machig Labdron who founded the *chod* lineage. He had a pupil there who had built a monastery.[31] It is here that Rechungpa's lineage was carried on unbroken. The pupils at Sangri said Rechungpa's teachings were very special and profound and requested him to sing a spiritual song that contained the essential meaning of the view of meditation. Rechungpa sang:

> If one doesn't understand the actual nature of appearances, then one is going to continue in samsara. If one does realize the nature of appearances, then one knows them to be the dharmakaya and there isn't any need to look for any other view.
> If one doesn't know how to rest the mind in meditation, then one has to meditate on the mind.

The mind has three characteristics which are luminosity, awareness, and emptiness. Luminosity means that there is an unbroken continuum of the mind. Awareness means one knows exactly what it is that one is doing. Emptiness means the mind has no true, solid reality. If one doesn't understand these three characteristics, many different thoughts will arise.

However, if one is able to rest in a natural, uncontrived state, this is the *sambhogakaya*.

As for conduct, one should just deal with whatever occurs and be totally natural without any fixed plan or system. This is called "naturally appearing" and "naturally liberating conduct."

It was at this time that Rechungpa while he was in his room had a direct vision of what is called the "lords of the three families." The lords of the three families are Manjushri, Avalokiteshvara, and Vajrapani. The three families are: Manjushri, the embodiment of all the wisdom of all the buddhas; Avalokiteshvara, the embodiment of the compassion of all the buddhas; and Vajrapani the embodiment of the power of all the buddhas. So Rechungpa saw these deities directly and he also saw Padmasambhava. Having seen them directly, he felt great happiness.

4. SIMOTRAK

Rechungpa then when on to Simotrak, which had many different texts on sorcery. Realizing these teachings could actually harm or injure other sentient beings, he decided that the best thing to do would be to hide them as terma, or treasure texts, until the time was appropriate for the texts to be used. These texts were entrusted to certain spirits, nonhumans, who were told to guard these teachings, and only give them to appropriate persons at the appropriate times.

During his practice one day, Rechungpa had a vision of Padmasambhava surrounded by four dakinis. He was so overjoyed at this vision he spontaneously sang a song:

In between the actual words of the Buddha and the commentaries are the oral instructions of how to practice. These instructions are extremely wondrous.

In between the scriptures and the logical expositions are the experiences of great bliss. I am very fortunate to have these.

I am able to dwell in the mountain solitude and retreats, and here my meditation experiences have increased greatly. Therefore, I have nothing but disgust for worldly activities.

In between this life and the next life are the wondrous oral instructions of the bardo. With these instructions, I can attain enlightenment in one lifetime.

In between my chest and my back are the subtle drops, channels, and winds. With this practice of the subtle channels and winds, the blessings can enter into my body.

If one doesn't have a realization like this, then it makes little sense to be a great meditator.

Here at Simotrak, many disciples came and Rechungpa was able to benefit many beings.

5. Mukpa

Rechungpa also gave many teachings on the mandala of Vajrapani. At this time Rechungpa had a dream in which he saw a mandala. This dream mandala had offerings on it and he realized that this was a sign. Milarepa in his prophecy said that there were five places Rechungpa should go to. The fifth place was Mukpa and Rechungpa thought that this was a sign from the dakinis for him to go to Mukpa. He sang a song to his pupils about that. Then using his cotton robe as wings, he flew to Mukpa which was over toward the high snow mountains.

After Rechungpa had flown to Mukpa, he went very high up in the snows to a very solitary place where no one ever went. None of Rechungpa's pupils knew where he was, so they went around trying to find him. It took them a very long time before they finally located him in a cave high up in the mountain. They were very happy to find him again after such a long time. They stayed with him receiving dharma teachings.

Rechungpa was in retreat here, but because he had become very famous as a highly accomplished master, many people came to request teachings from him. One day, when he was giving instructions on Mahamudra, he felt great delight, and therefore sang a song about how very fortunate he was:

I am very fortunate because: first, I have a precious human birth. Second, not only do I have a precious human birth, but I was able to meet with the dharma. Third, not only was I able to meet with the dharma, but I was able to study and contemplate it, and, therefore, resolve all doubts about the dharma. In this way, definite certainty and confidence arose in me.

I was also fortunate in another way: first, I was able to develop renunciation from samsaric confusion. Second, having developed renunciation, I was able to abandon all worldly activity. Third, I was able to attend a guru endowed with meditative experience and realization. In this way too, I was very fortunate. Therefore, based on these three reasons, not only have I understood the dharma, but I have been able to attain success on the path.

I have had many benefits from the special meditations I have practiced: first, I was able to receive the transmissions of the oral lineage; second, not only did I receive the transmission of the oral lineage, but I was able to see the true nature of mind directly, without any fabrication; and, third based on practicing this in my meditation, the realization of non-meditation arose in my mind. Based on this realization, I experience no distinction between meditation and postmeditation.

Therefore, my meditation is unceasing. The reason that it is unceasing is: first, I am continuously inseparable from meditation itself; second, I have no attachment to this life; and third, having realized this, all external appearances arise as meditation. Having seen the true nature of mind, all appearances that arise for the mind arise as meditation.

I also have great confidence based on this realization. The reasons are: first, I have been able to overpower and attain mastery over all discursive thought; second, the wisdom of great bliss has arisen in my being; and third, I have realized the true nature of mind, which is beyond separation or attainment, beyond accomplishment and refutation. Therefore, in this way, I have great confidence in my realization, and I do not need to ask anyone else about how my meditation is.

At this point then, there is no reason for me not to die: first, I am able to meditate continuously day and night; second, experiences of realization have arisen in my mind; and third, I have realized the true nature of reality, which is beyond all concept.

I have been able to establish disciples on the path of enlightenment. First, I have received the blessings of a very special guru. Second, not only have I received his blessings, but I have also received his prophecy that in the future this would help a great many beings. Third, not only have I received his blessings and his prophecy, but also the benefit to these beings has been spontaneous and effortless.

Rechungpa then transmitted the power of his experience, his realization, and his compassion to his students, saying, "May this occur in you as well."

It was also in Mukpa where Rechungpa met Jawa Lo who was to become his main student. At this time there were many, many disciples who had gathered around Rechungpa. Rechungpa became a little overwhelmed by all these people, so, he and Jawa Lo went into retreat. During this retreat very special experiences and realizations arose in Jawa Lo. In particular, he was able to resolve all doubts concerning the practice of the winds and the channels.

While Jawa Lo was practicing this meditation, he had an experience where, in the space in front of him, many bodhisattvas appeared, and he heard the sounds of different kinds of music being played. He went to Rechungpa, and asked him, "What is this? What do these experiences mean?

Rechungpa replied, "This is a sign that the subtle wind, has entered into the central channel, however, it seems like your subtle wind is still a little bit rough."

Jawa Lo then asked Rechungpa, "What is the difference between rough subtle wind and soft subtle wind?"

Rechungpa then explained, "The subtle wind cannot be too rough, or too hard. For example, if you are irrigating a field, and the water becomes too cold, it will cause problems in irrigating the field. In terms of subtle wind, there are two kinds of prana: the upper prana and the lower prana. When you are holding the upper prana, you need to hold all of it, whereas, you need to hold only two-thirds of the lower prana."

Having been given the instructions on the inner heat practice, the illusory body practice, the dream practice, and the luminosity practice, Jawa Lo became an extraordinary student.

RECHUNGPA'S ACCOMPLISHMENTS

Rechungpa had a retreat center on top of a mountain. This was a very wonderful place because by staying there and practicing, meditation experience developed greatly. So he felt very fortunate to have stayed in this place.

One accomplishment that he had was the accumulation of merit and the accumulation of wisdom which is essential for the attainment of Buddhahood. These two accumulations serve to establish nondualistic compassion, which when developed is wonderful. The sign that one's compassion is nondualistic and not compassion still concerned with "I" and "other" appears in one's inner meditation, not externally. Therefore Rechungpa didn't need to make any physical effort of body or speech to develop this kind of compassion. It just appeared naturally from his own inner realization.

While Rechungpa was going to the sacred places and singing spiritual songs, he gave many meditation instructions. He also had instructions on sorcery. If these instructions on sorcery had fallen into the wrong hands, they could have brought harm to other beings.

Rechungpa therefore concealed them in a rock cliff in a rocky mountain as a *dharma treasure* (Tib. *terma*). He entrusted these to a spirit who lived in that area saying, "Guard these teachings so that they don't fall into the wrong hands and cause harm to others. Some time in the future when a person of good karmic fortune appears, give him these instructions."[32]

Then Rechungpa went to a solitary place to practice and during his practice he had a vision of Vajradhara encircled by Indian *mahasiddhas*. Having received this vision, his meditation developed and deepened and he became steeped in samadhi and remained for several days in this meditative state. When he finally emerged from it, he felt great joy.

Chapter 9

Latchi Repents

R echungpa concealed the teachings on sorcery as a treasure to be discovered in the future. He also had a vision of the Kagyu lineage which made him very happy and in his happiness he sang this song. His pupils said that their guru Rechungpa's songs were powerful and had very great blessing. Hearing even just some of the words would cause a change in people's experience so they requested him to sing them a song. Rechungpa sang:

I am a yogi and the song that I composed comes from my own experience. You should listen very carefully without distraction to this song and keep it in your mind.

The lineage I hold is the lineage of meditation instructions that benefit the mind. If these meditation instructions were taken away by the mouth of reasoning, it would be a great loss.

If we look at our body externally, it is an *illusory body*. It has no longevity, but in fact it is the body from which the body of the Buddha arises. Since it is the foundation from which the body of the Buddha arises, we shouldn't just see it as an ordinary body. We should meditate on it as the body of a deity. To see our body as the body of a deity is very important.

If one has the instructions of the *path of means*, one shouldn't just listen to these instructions without using them. This would be a great waste. Instead, one should apply oneself with diligence to this path of means and follow the instructions.

RECHUNGPA BURIES MORE TERMA

In accordance with Milarepa's prophecy, Rechungpa went again to the Yarlung Valley. In the Yarlung Valley there is the mountain, Yarlha Shampo, and this mountain looks like an upside down *kapala,* or a human skullcap. This is said to be a special place for Chakrasamvara and a place where one can receive very great blessings from doing the Chakrasamvara practice. Milarepa had told Rechungpa that he should go there and practice Chakrasamvara and if he did, he would gain a special pupil.

While practicing there, he had a vision of Tibupa. Tibupa was dressed in charnel ground adornment and accompanied by many dakinis. Tibupa said to him that at present there was no one practicing the instructions of *one taste* and so it would be best if he were to hide these instructions as a *terma* for the future. So Rechungpa went close to the south of Tibet where there is a very deep ravine and many special caves and there he concealed the teachings on one taste for a *terton* to find in the future. After Rechungpa had a vision of Vajrapani in the form of a garuda, he concealed the teachings of one taste in a place called Lhodrak Kharchu. There was a local female deity there called Genyen Chonkha. Rechungpa said to Genyen Chonkha, "You must guard these teachings for seven generations. In the future there will come someone called Lorepa. When Lorepa comes, you must give him these teachings. Until that time don't give them to anyone else and keep them a secret." So he entrusted the teaching to her with that command.

WHAT HAD BECOME OF LATCHI

Meanwhile Latchi's father, the ruler of Yarlung, was angry at her for her poor behavior to Rechungpa. To punish her, he said, "I'm going to give you to the first person who comes tomorrow to the palace and you will have to leave this land." So that night Latchi prayed very hard that the first person to come the next day would be handsome, rich, and important. She must have had some bad karma because the first person to come was a leper. So her father gave her to the leper and she was exiled from Yarlung. She had a very hard time being a servant for this leper and had to go around from place to place begging for food. During this time she also caught leprosy. She asked several lamas for the best thing to do. One lama made a prophecy. He said that she must have done something very bad to a special teacher and broken her samaya commitment to him. He said, "Ideally the best thing you could do is to find him and make a confession. If you can't do that, you should do the practice of Vajrapani. If you can't even do that, at the very least, you should go to the place called Nyalmay and circumambulate the stupa there." So Latchi and her husband decided the best thing to do would be to go to Rechungpa. She knew the spiritual commitments she had to him and how she had mistreated him. Rechungpa also had the Vajrapani instructions so if they could meet him, he could give them the instructions that could cure their leprosy. Thus they went searching for Rechungpa.

They were told that Rechungpa was living at Yarlha Shampo mountain. They went there but when they arrived, he had already left. People said, "Oh, he was here but he left." Latchi and her husband were very upset but went on to Nyalmay which was nearby to circumambulate the stupa. A discouraged Latchi lay face down on the grass and thought, "Well, I used to be a princess. I used to have gold and turquoise jewelry. I had beautiful clothes made of silk and brocade. I used to have a good horse to ride and I could eat whenever I wanted and now look at the state I'm in!" She got more and more depressed and upset.

While Latchi was lying there, some merchants came by, one was saying, "I came to sell my things but it didn't work out. I haven't been able to accomplish what I intended, so I'm going to give up being a merchant and I'm going to practice the dharma. I'm going to go to a valley called Loro where there's a pupil of Milarepa called Rechungpa. I've made up my mind to practice dharma with him." Latchi heard him and when she heard Rechungpa's name she thought, "So now I know where he is!"

Latchi went to the merchant and said to him, "Where is this place where Rechungpa is staying and how long is he staying there?" The merchant replied, "You must be going around with a pot over your head. You don't know anything! Everybody knows Rechungpa. He is famous! He's staying in Loro and I'm going there because I've been beating my donkey a lot for no purpose." "Well, how far is it?" she asked. He replied, "If you go by donkey it's three days but if you walk on your own it will only take you one day!"

So she told her husband, "You stay here and circumambulate the stupa. I'll go to see Rechungpa and confess to him and then I'll come back. If I find him and confess to him, we'll both be cured." Her husband agreed saying, "Yes, that's a very good idea. You go find Rechungpa and confess to him."

RECHUNGPA TEACHES LATCHI A LESSON

This time Rechungpa was giving teachings in a cave. He knew that Latchi was coming and he told his pupils, "Today there is someone coming who broke her dharma commitments. So when this person comes throw dirt on her and mistreat her and pour abuse on her. The reason is that she has accumulated some bad karma and feels very great regret and unhappiness about it. So if you do it, she will be purified." Rechungpa went back to his room and stayed there.

Latchi arrived and started coming up to where Rechungpa was living. She saw his pupil Rinchen Drak who had been living with Rechungpa in Yarlung. When she saw him, she started crying and saying, "You and Rechungpa went off, just leaving me. I've had such a hard time. But I've come to confess to him so would you help me to do that?" Rinchen Drak said, "It will be very difficult for you to go and make this confession so I'll help you." He went up with her and as they got closer all of Rechungpa's pupils began throwing dirt and stones at her. Rinchen Drak pleaded, "No, No! Don't do this! She lived with Rechungpa a long time. Her family gave him everything. They lived and ate their food together and everything. So please stop throwing stones at her! We need to meet with Rechungpa."

Then Rinchen Drak went up to see Rechungpa and said, "Latchi has arrived and wants to confess to you. Will you let her come?" And Rechungpa said, "No, she can't come and make confession to me. She likes turquoise so much. I have some turquoise and gold so you go and give it to her and tell her to go away. She has broken her dharma commitments so she can't do dharma practice. There's nothing to be done."

Rinchen Drak went back down and said, "He told me to give you this turquoise and gold. It's best that you don't come and see him." Latchi said, "I don't want the turquoise and gold. I used to live in a palace and I had plenty of gold and turquoise and it didn't do me any good. It is not permanent so I don't want it. If I can't go and confess to him, I'll kill myself. It's better than living out this awful life!" So Rinchen Drak went back up to see Rechungpa and Rechungpa said, "If she really wants to make this confession, she should recite the one-hundred syllable mantra of Vajrasattva and get a stupa and a statue of the Buddha made. If she does that then she will be able to make an actual confession for what she has done." When this message was taken to her, Latchi was so happy to hear it, she went away and did it all. She said the mantra and had the stupa and statue built. Having done all this she was able to meet with Rechungpa.

When Latchi met with him, Rechungpa sang her a song:

I always think of the kindness of my guru Milarepa. You should know that the turquoise piece over which we quarreled was on the mandala in Milarepa's cave. When I saw it, all the hairs on my body stood on end and I felt very great faith and devotion in him.

In the beginning Milarepa told me not to go to central Tibet and then later on he told me I must go. When I think of him, I think of how very amazing and wonderful he is.

For Milarepa earth, mud, and gold were exactly the same. But when I was leaving for central Tibet, he insisted that I take this gold with me.

The reason he asked me to take the gold was so I could now give it to you. If you use this gold to make stupas and statues of the Buddha, it will purify your negative karma and the obscurations of your body. You can use it to get mantras written to purify your speech and you can use it to get a *tsa tsa* made to purify your mind.

If you will do all this, I will give you dharma instructions.

Latchi had already made one statue and one stupa as purification in order to meet him and now she had to do others to receive Rechungpa's actual instructions. After she finished these acts of contrition, she and her husband received the empowerments and instructions of Vajrapani. By doing this practice she was cured of leprosy. Not only were Latchi and her husband cured, but all their leper friends were also cured. After practicing for seven or eight years, Latchi herself attained the accomplishments of a siddha so that when she passed away her body became *sacred relics*. She became a great meditator.

Chapter 10

Rechungpa's Final Days

There was a man called Dawa Drakpa who was extremely ill and dying. He requested that Rechungpa come and see him. So Rechungpa went to help the man and gave him teachings on refuge, bodhichitta as well as the bardo instructions. The man said that when he died, he wanted Rechungpa to have his house, all his possessions, and his wife. Rechungpa said "Oh no! I can't look after all these things because I have left behind home and wife. I've given all that up, so I can't look after them." The man said "I can't just die and leave my wife behind so I'll kill her before I die." Rechungpa said, "Oh well! In that case, I'll take these things." So he got the house and married the man's wife.[33]

MILAREPA'S DEATH

Rechungpa continued giving teachings to his pupils. While Rechungpa was practicing in strict retreat, one night at midnight, his state of sleep and the state of luminosity mixed together so that he had a vision of Milarepa at Lachi Truwar. He saw a crystal stupa being lifted up into the sky by a host of dakinis who were paying homage to it. There were also many gods and goddesses who were making offerings to the stupa. Rechungpa prostrated and circumambulated it. Milarepa's face appeared in the stupa and said to Rechungpa, "Please come and see me. We have to meet." Milarepa was very happy and joyous. At this point Rechungpa awoke and remembered the dream and thought, "My guru is entering parinirvana." At this point two women appeared and said to him, "Please

85

come quickly. If you don't, you will not be able to meet with your guru."

The cockerels were crowing as it was the beginning of the day. It was actually a two months journey to Guntang, the place where Milarepa was but through his practice of holding his inner air, he got there by the next sunrise. When Rechungpa arrived, he saw many rainbow lights in the sky and had an experience of seeing many strange clouds. There were a lot of male and female deities doing prostrations. When he saw this, he felt a mixture of happiness and sadness and he thought, "Maybe this means that Milarepa has passed away and he is no longer alive." Sitting in meditation he met a goddess and he asked her, "What is the reason for all these signs and omens?" She said to him, "Are you going around with your eyes and ears covered? Don't you know that Milarepa is going to the pure realms? We are making offerings to him."

Rechungpa then set off immediately to reach Milarepa's cave and on the way, close to the cave, was a great rock. As he arrived, he saw Milarepa sitting on top of this rock. It was like a visionary experience. Rechungpa thought "Milarepa is still alive! They told me that he has died but he hasn't! Here he is!" and he prostrated to him and supplicated him and Milarepa said to him, "Don't come straight away, follow me afterwards. I'll go ahead of you and prepare a welcome for you." Then Milarepa disappeared.

When Rechungpa finally reached the cave, there were offerings being made and at the entrance to the cave there were some new pupils of Milarepa who wouldn't let Rechungpa in. They said, "No, you can't go in! New people are not allowed into the cave." Of course, they didn't recognize Rechungpa. Rechungpa felt very sad and upset because Milarepa was in there dying and he couldn't meet with him because the newer generation of Milarepa's pupils were not letting him into the cave. So he sang a supplication to Milarepa.

The funeral pyre was on fire when Rechungpa arrived, and the students saw Milarepa holding down the flames with his hands and singing a song.

When the cremation pyre was lit the smoke and flames formed various shapes and forms in the sky. The fire was forming into the eight auspicious symbols and the smoke formed into offering god-desses and mandalas. Seeing these shapes the people thought, "When the cremation is over there will be many sacred relics contained in the pyre and many special objects." So they spent the night circled around the cremation pyre.

While they were sleeping, Rechungpa had a dream that the five classes of dakinis came carrying silk cloth and in this cloth they took away all of the sacred relics. When he woke up, he called to all the other yogis saying "Quick, go and open the cremation pyre!" They opened it, looked inside, and it was completely empty; there weren't even any ashes left. Everything had been taken by the dakinis.

Then Rechungpa sang a song of supplication to the dakinis say-ing that he needed to have some special objects of Milarepa to make special offerings and prayers to. But the dakinis from space called back down and said that the disciples had the special samadhi and the supreme accomplishments given to them by Milarepa so they didn't need any relics. It was the dakinis that needed something to make an offering to and they said, "So we're not going to give you any!"

The disciples ended up without any relics except for Milarepa's robe and his staff. These few things that he wore were kept as relics and divided among his pupils. Rechungpa took charge in giving advice to the pupils and he told them what they should do and how they should practice.

At that time Gampopa was in Central Tibet and had not been able to come for Milarepa's death and cremation. The staff and robe were to be given to Gampopa so Rechungpa set off to meet Gampopa and give him these things. Since they were the two main pupils of Milarepa, they went to Rechungpa's residence and there they went through all of the instructions that they had received from Milarepa and checked them. They did this, working together in harmony checking the instructions they had received from Milarepa to see that they were complete. After going through them and checking them, they organized them.

During that time some of his pupils were not acting in accordance with the dharma so Rechungpa said to them:

We are all very fortunate and so we shouldn't have these differing views and negative conduct. There is a marketplace full of gurus but we have been able to study with the very best guru, Milarepa. There is a great marketplace full of instructions but we have the best which are the instructions of the oral practice lineage. There is a large market full of meditations but we have the best which is the Six Yogas of Naropa. So having the best teacher, instructions, and meditations we are indeed fortunate. At this time we should not be involved in wrong views and activities.

All of his pupils were able to follow the dharma properly and they became very good pupils and many became very accomplished.

MEETING OF RECHUNGPA AND DUSUM KHYENPA

One night when Rechungpa was asleep, he dreamt that an extremely ugly woman appeared to him and said, "An emanation is going to come and see you," then she disappeared. After that Dusum Khyenpa, the first Karmapa came from Kham, in eastern Tibet. Dusum Khyenpa had many special signs and had previously met Gampopa and received meditation instructions from him. Gampopa had about eight hundred great meditators among his students, but among them Dusum Khyenpa had the greatest skill and the greatest diligence in meditation. Now he had come to see Rechungpa.

The meeting between Dusum Khyenpa and Rechungpa occurred in Tsong in the western part of Central Tibet. There he received from Rechungpa instructions on the Six Yogas of Naropa, instructions on the Mahamudra and in particular, the red instructions and the oral instructions of Maitripa on Mahamudra. He also received special instructions on eliminating obstacles and hindrances.

Rechungpa told him that he must come to see him where he was staying. So the Karmapa did that and was given the empowerment to the mandala of Chakrasamvara and through this he gained great realization and power. For example, when a lightening flash struck, by

88

doing the pointing mudra with his hands he was able to make the lightening turn around and go back up.

RECHUNGPA'S PASSING AWAY

At the end of his life, Rechungpa told his pupils that all worldly things are impermanent and he also was impermanent so they should receive all of the instructions that Rechungpa possessed, without any left out. So they did this and he taught all of the instructions that he knew. Then to some pupils he said, "You must practice this particular practice and having practiced it, you must spread this teaching to other pupils." To another person he said, "You must do this practice and spread this to other people." So he gave everyone individual advice on what they should do.

At this point, Rechungpa's spiritual biography has the names of a number of different pupils. It gives their names and what practices they were to do, and how they should spread the teaching. We will skip these details for now.

At this time Rechungpa said his activity was completed. All the pupils that he needed to help and train had been helped and there was no one left to train. It was time to help people in another place and begin working elsewhere. Then the news started spreading that Rechungpa was going to pass away. So they said to him, "What should we do? What pure realm are you going to go to and what should we do with your body? How should we do the cremation and what offerings should we make?" Rechungpa answered, "As I've attained and realized the dharmakaya it doesn't really make any difference what pure realm you pray to. Because my body has become the mandala of the deity, when I die there won't be any body so you won't have to light any fires for the cremation."

Rechungpa then said, "I have given you my dharma teachings, you have received and are practicing them, so I will never be apart from you." He went into his own room and was in a state of great happiness. Many offerings were set out, and his students did a *ganachakra* feast offering together right in the middle of the night. When this feast was over, Rechungpa said, "Now go back to your own individual rooms and meditate there. Tonight many lights, sounds, and so on will happen, but whatever happens, don't come out to look at me. You must all just stay where you are and meditate."

At daybreak, all sorts of sounds and music and flutes and lights appeared from space, and the smell of perfume pervaded everywhere. There was also an earthquake or an earth tremor. All the pupils in their caves had been told by Rechungpa that whatever happens, they should just stay in their rooms and meditate and not look, but they went out just to have a tiny, little peek, outside. In the sky, they could sometimes see dakinis: sometimes half a dakini, sometimes a whole dakini. Sometimes they could see Rechungpa there in the sky as well, sometimes appearing as Chakrasamvara, sometimes as different things and these appearances kept going higher and higher into the sky.

At daybreak, all the pupils went to Rechungpa's cave and found that their teacher was gone and there was no sign of him. All that was left was his clothes and his seat. He had gone to the pure realms without leaving any physical body behind. He hadn't died in the ordinary way through becoming ill, gradually dying, and then becoming a corpse, but died without any sign of illness. He immediately left to the pure realms.

All of the pupils that day sang spiritual songs or made supplications and prayers to Rechungpa. During that day there came from space, although there was no form to be seen, a voice saying, "If you pray to the pure realm of Vajrapani, you will receive Rechungpa's blessings." So all the people gathered together and did supplications and prayers to Rechungpa and preserved all of the teachings that he had given them. They maintained and practiced them, and they transmitted them to others, so that all of Rechungpa's teachings were able to spread and continue.

RECHUNGPA'S LINEAGE

Originally the teachings of Rechungpa were passed on by his pupils. Later on, a separate tradition of Rechungpa ceased to exist. What happened was that lamas of other traditions received these teachings and so his teachings and instructions spread through other traditions, particularly the Karma Kagyu and the Drukpa Kagyu schools. The First Drukchen Rinpoche, Tsangpa Gyare passed the oral instructions of Rechungpa into the Drukpa Kagyu lineage. Dusum Khyenpa, the first Karmapa, passed them onto the Karma Kagyu lineage.

In this biography, we have found that Rechungpa encountered a great number of obstacles and difficult situations. For example, he was stopped from going to Milarepa's cave when he was dying by Milarepa's newer students. So we hear about these obstacles, but the main point of this story is that of meditational accomplishment, of the oral instructions, and how when he died, he just entered the pure realms. This just shows the power of dharma practice and the power of the oral instructions. If we can practice the dharma, then, as they say in Tibetan, "we create our own benefit." What we are doing in dharma practice is not for someone else, but we are trying to help ourselves and the person who can do that is us. So we have to help ourselves. If we wish to do that, then we should carefully practice the dharma.

Before Rechungpa passed away, many different kinds of signs and omens occurred. His pupils came and asked him what these signs meant. Rechungpa replied, "Well, for me they mean something really good, but who knows what it means for you." He knew he was going from a state of happiness and bliss to a state of even greater happiness and bliss. So this shows the power of the dharma. If we are able to practice the dharma, then we can also achieve this state.

Other books by Thrangu Rinpoche

The Three Vehicles of Buddhist Practice. An overview of the three levels of practice: the Hinayana, Mahayana, and Vajrayana. Boulder: Namo Buddha Publications, 1998.

The Middle-way Meditation Instructions of Mipham Rinpoche. This great scholar who actually stayed for a while with the previous Thrangu Rinpoche at his monastery describes how one develops compassion and then expands this into bodhichitta and eventually develops prajna or wisdom. Boulder: Namo Buddha Publications, 2000.

The Four Foundations of Buddhist Practice. There are four thoughts one should contemplate before practicing: precious human birth, impermanence, karma, and the drawbacks of samsara. Boulder: Namo Buddha Publications, 2001.

Transcending Ego: Distinguishing Consciousness from Wisdom. This book, which includes the original text of the Third Karmapa and Thrangu Rinpoche's commentary, describes in detail the eight consciousnesses and how these transform into the five wisdoms at enlightenment. It is a book on Buddhist psychology. Boulder: Namo Buddha Publications, 2001.

The Open Door to Emptiness. An easy-to-understand commentary by Rinpoche on the Middle-way arguments made to establish that all phenomena are indeed empty. Vancouver: Karme Thekchen Choling, 1997.

The Practice of Tranquillity and Insight. A practical and detailed guide on three important Buddhist meditations: Shamatha, Vipasyana, and Mahamudra. Ithaca: Snow Lion Publications, 1993.

Buddha Nature. An overview of the concept of Buddha-nature as it is presented in Maitreya's *Uttaratantra.* Kathmandu: Rangjung Yeshe Publications, 1993.

The Songs of Naropa. A telling of the life of Naropa and a detailed analysis of his famous Summary of Mahamudra which lays out the path of mahamudra meditation by the guru whose succession of students went on to found the Kagyu lineage. Kathmandu: Rangjung Yeshe Publications, 1997.

Showing the Path of Liberation. Thrangu Rinpoche was asked to outline the path to enlightenment by the Sixteenth Gyalwa Karmapa. He did so in this profound text which uses the Kagyu Lineage Prayer as an outline to the path. Namo Buddha and Zhyisil Chokyi Ghatsal Publications, 2001.

Notes

By Clark Johnson, Ph. D.
(Unless otherwise noted)

1. This is a special spiritual practice called rainbow body (Tib. *jal lu*) which can only be done by highly accomplished meditators. Traditionally, they ask to be sealed up in a tent at their time of death and are left alone for about a week. When the tent is opened up, only the nails and hair remain. This is still practiced today. For example, Achoe Rinpoche of Tibet achieved rainbow body in the 1990s.

2. The text that Thrangu Rinpoche used was Rechungpa's spiritual biography called, *The Radiance of Wisdom: The Clear Mirror of the Path to Omniscience and Liberation* by Gotsang Repa. This text which is about 200 pages long has not been translated into English.

3. The Tibetans believe that if one angers a naga spirit, one will develop a skin disease such as leprosy. The cure which is done even in modern times involving a lama doing a ceremony to appease the naga.

4. This is a special practice called a dark retreat. One stays in complete darkness meditating for a period of time in order to see the clear light of the mind.

5. The first teacher of Rechungpa was Walatsendra in the kingdom of Tirhut which was transcribed in the Tibetan Tengyur as Balacandra. The eastern dialect in India pronounces the 'v' as 'b' and pronounces the 'r' as an 'l,' so they say 'laja' instead of 'raja' for example. This was also the Buddha's dialect as can be demonstrated by the Ashokan inscriptions at Lumbini. So actually his teacher's name was Varacandra. —*Peter Roberts*

6. Vajrapani is one of the three main protectors. He is especially associated with curing illnesses caused by nagas. Vajrapani became a main yidam for Rechungpa.

93

7. See Thrangu Rinpoche's *Ten Teachings from the 100,000 Songs of Milarepa* (Boulder: Namo Buddha Publications, 1999) for a description of this contest in which each side produced miracles until Milarepa finally did a miracle that the Bonpo master could not duplicate and thus Mount Kailash became a Buddhist area.

8. Because of Milarepa's realization of bodhichitta, he knew the consequences of using sorcery. However, ordinary Tibetans of that time would have never taken the chance.

9. Rinpoche has explained elsewhere that beginning students should follow the form of making prayers, developing devotion, and doing the preliminary practices. Later on, when they have developed spiritual realization and experiences the emptiness of phenomena, they can go beyond the form by observing the mind directly which is the Dzogchen and Mahamudra approach to meditation.

10. A meditational deity (or yidam in Tibetan) is a deity such as Vajrasattva, Hevajra, or Chakrasamvara towards whom the practitioner feels a special connection. When practice is not going well, the practitioner can pray to this deity and ask for blessings. The yidam, like all other deities, are expressions of an outer form as well as a manifestation of inner experience.

11. There are still many stories about zombies called "rolongs" among Tibetans. It is said that if a rolong touches you, you turn into a rolong. Also they cannot bend down so many Tibetan and Nepalese houses have a low door which makes bending necessary to enter the house.

12. This story is also told in *The Life of Marpa*. Boston: Shambhala Publications, 1982.

13. The Tibetans typically cut up the corpse in pieces and feed them to vultures.

14. Tilopa was the first to obtain the formless dakini teachings. Having traveled to Uddiyana, he received them directly from the formless wisdom dakini in a spiritual song. Basically, this song was comprised of these nine instructions: (1) Loose the seal knot of mind as ripening and freeing (Tib. *smin-grol sems kyi rgya-mdud shig*), (2) Look at the mirror of mind as samaya (Tib. *dam-*

tshig rang-sems me-long ltos), (3) Slash water with a sword as activity (Tib. *spyod-pa chu Ia ral-gri rgyob*), (4) Sun yourself in realization as samaya substance (Tib. *dam rdzas rtogs-pa'i nyi-ma 'des*), (5) Look at the torch of wisdom as insight (Tib. *rig-pa ye-shes sgron-me ltos*), (6) Turn the wheel of the web.of nadi and prana (Tib. *rtsa rlung dra-mig 'khor-lo skor*), (7) Look at the outer mirror as equal taste (Tib. *ro-snyoms phyi yi me-long ltos*), (8) Meditate on self-liberated mahamudra (Tib. *rang-grol phyag-rgya chen-po sgoms*), and (9) Hold the jewel of the great bliss teachings (Tib. *bde-chen gsung gi rin-chen zungs*).

—From *The Life of Marpa, the Translator*, p. 176.

15. This practice of swift feet (Tib. *kang gyok*) is described by Alexandra David-Neel in *Magic and Mystery in Tibet*. The meditator takes a phurba and points it in the chosen direction and begins walking, almost running, without stopping or diverting from the path for days at a time.

16. Rinpoche has explained in other teachings that once one reaches the meditative state that truly realizes emptiness, then solid objects are truly empty and one can pass through them. Modern physics tells us this is entirely possible because solid matter is actually over 99.99% space with the atoms being enormous distances between each other on an atomic level.

17. Chenrezig, the deity of compassion, has had a number of emanations including Songtsen Gampo, Padmasambhava, the Dalai Lamas, and the Gyalwa Karmapas. Naropa foretold that there would be five special tantras that would go to Tibet and this one would be brought to Tibet by a student of Marpa. These teachings were given to Khandro Karpa Sangpo to Tibupa who passed them on to Rechungpa. Rechungpa taught these to Dusum Khyenpa. Dusum Khyenpa practiced the high Red Chenrezig and later become known as the first Karmapa. This particular practice is with Red Chenrezig in union with a consort.

18. There are two kinds of dakinis—human and nonhuman. The human dakinis are realized female practitioners and the nonhuman dakinis are wisdom beings that appear to help the practitioner. It should be noted that two highly realized women dakinis

played an important part in Rechungpa's life. The dakini who corrected the translations which have been passed down for generations and Machig Drupe Jalmo who literally saved Rechungpa's life and gave him the Amitayus and the Red Chenrezig sadhana which are still practiced in the Kagyu lineage.

19. They carried the old woman away and did the phowa (transfer of consciousness) practice and then left her up in a high empty place where she'd be eaten by the birds. If she were left among the people, someone could have come along and claimed her body.

To explain further, when someone dies the mind leaves the body and there are many exits from which the mind can leave. At the time of death one has the experience of being inside a ruined house and so one thinks, "I have to get out of this place!" One can see many, many exits, some above and some below and so on. The exit that the mind takes will determine what kind of rebirth. For example, leaving through the nose will result in a rebirth as a human being and leaving through the anus one is reborn in the hell realm and so on. So the phowa practice is designed so that the consciousness will exit from the body through this opening at the top of the head leading to a good rebirth. On the ultimate level of reality wherever one looks, inside or outside, one cannot find the mind. On the relative level of reality there is a mind and so this mind dwells in the body.

There are two kinds of phowa. The first is where one practices and then at the time of death through the power of one's practice one actually sends the consciousness out of a particular opening in the body. Second is when a teacher who is accomplished in meditation and visualization helps someone who dies. He does the visualization and through love and compassion he helps the dead person's consciousness leave through the crown of the head. In the Varjayana tradition when someone dies, one can invite a special lama to come and do the phowa for them. But in this case the old lady had never done any phowa practice so it was Milarepa who was doing it through the power of his great compassion.

But phowa practice can't change one's karma. The old woman's karma didn't cease to exist. But sometimes, through certain conditions one can change one's karma. For example, one might have bad karma and then one meets a great teacher and through that positive condition, one can eliminate one's bad karma. Or one can meet negative conditions and on top of the bad karma one starts accumulating more bad karma. It could have happened that this old woman had good and bad karma and through having Milarepa do phowa practice for her, her good karma would bring a good rebirth. Through that rebirth she would be able to practice the dharma and purify her bad karma. You have two factors. You have karma from the past and you have present conditions. So this is a case of the power of present conditions and circumstances.

—Thrangu Rinpoche

20. There are channels in the body similar to meridians in acupuncture which are not anatomical. These channels carry energy or "winds" which when controlled with meditation and Varjayana practices can lead to yogic powers.

21. I believe the problem of pride is probably the same in the West as in the East. For example, Rechungpa was a very special pupil with a good practice, but sometimes his pride rose as an obstacle. So it's something that one has to eliminate. The way of eliminating the pride is to understand selflessness, the absence of self. If one can realize that, then pride will naturally be eliminated. Also being aware of and understanding one's own faults and shortcomings will eliminate pride.

In the visualization practices during the *creation phase*, one has to have the qualities such as clarity, mindfulness and pride. There has to be unshakable pride called vajra pride which means that one thinks of oneself as the deity. So that whatever deity one is practicing—Avalokiteshvara or Vajrasattva or Padmasambhava— one thinks, "I am the deity." One really has to think this and so this is called unshakable pride. Also in terms of dharma practice one thinks, "I can practice the dharma, I'm able to do it." This kind of pride called vajra pride is good and necessary.

—Thrangu Rinpoche

22. Rechungpa's dream of shouting three times in three different valleys was a sign that he had disobeyed his teacher three times and that he would be reborn three times as a great scholar. He disobeyed his teacher, but did not break his vajrayana commitments (samaya vows).

—Thrangu Rinpoche

23. Being involved with the eight worldly dharmas is a way of thinking. It is a mental condition which is classified as a form of attachment. It's feeling pleasure and displeasure in things. They are actually four opposite emotions, namely: (a) If one acquires something, one feels pleased; if one doesn't acquire it, one feels displeased. (b) If one is praised, one is pleased; if one is not praised, one is displeased. (c) If one feels happy, one is pleased; if one feels unhappy, one is displeased. (d) If one is famous, one is pleased; if one isn't famous, one is displeased. These make up the eight worldly dharmas. Involvement with them will cause obstacles to one's dharma practice. It is being attached to the acquisition of objects, wanting to be happy, praised, and famous that will cause obstacles to one's spiritual practice.

—Thrangu Rinpoche

24. This practice and instruction on the subtle channels is a special Vajrayana technique. To do this practice one needs to have a foundation of the view and meditation. If there is this foundation and one receives the instructions and practices them, eventually this practice becomes powerful and effective. Whereas, if one receives these instructions and doesn't have a good foundation of the view and meditation, one won't receive any benefit from doing the practice on the subtle channels and winds. It's like playing a game and no one ever wins.

Because one needs to have the view and meditation, teachers give the instructions of channels and airs only to those who have this foundation. To those who don't, they don't give the instructions because it wouldn't really be of any benefit to them. But if one is practicing to receive the right view and meditation, then one will eventually receive these teachings and practice them.

The eighth Karmapa, Mikyo Dorje said, "The Kagyu lamas

these days are not achieving Buddhahood. If the Kagyu lamas were to achieve Buddhahood, then balloons would also achieve Buddhahood because if you blow up a balloon you'll fill it full of air and that's all the Kagyu lamas are doing. They are all sitting there practicing filling themselves up with air.

—Thrangu Rinpoche

(Note) This was a criticism of the lamas simply practicing the vase breathing part of the Six Yogas of Naropa, instead of doing a full Mahamudra practice. In vase breathing one forces air into the abdomen and holds it there as long as possible in an attempt to force the wind into the central channel. —CJ

25. This is a Tibetan practice of accumulating auspicious connections. One asks a lama who isn't one's teacher to give a teaching so that there will be a karmic bond there. Then in a later lifetime one has a better chance of meeting that teacher.

26. There are six realms of samsara: those of gods, jealous gods, humans, animals, hungry ghosts, and beings in the hell realms. Rinpoche says these are real, actual realms and in the early days bodhisattvas used to go to these realms and come back and describe them.

27. Tsurpu in Tibet is about 20 miles north of Lhasa and is where the Karmapas resided, including the present 17th Karmapa until he escaped from Tibet in January of 2000.

28. Rechungpa's monastery, Rechungpuk, is very close to Yomo Lhakang which is the oldest building in Tibet located in the Yarlung Valley. I went there when I was very little but I don't remember it very clearly or where they are in relation to each other. First Rechungpa went to live in the Yarlung Valley and he had Rechungpuk built. After that he crossed the Tsangpo River and headed straight for Nyanang where Milarepa was. When he went to Yarlung, he visited Lhasa and Samye Temple and Phenpo which is a valley near Lhasa which is called Tsumtrong in the text. This is where he went to see the Nepalese master Asu.

—Thrangu Rinpoche

29. Milarepa sent him to central Tibet saying it would be beneficial but there would be a danger of being bitten by a female dog. He

arrived in central Tibet alone. Then he took Princess Latchi as his consort and this eventually became an obstacle to his practice. Milarepa had emanated as a beggar and Rechungpa had given him the turquoise. So, through him having given the turquoise to the emanation of Milarepa he became free of these adverse circumstances.
—Thrangu Rinpoche

30. Samye Monastery is the first Buddhist Monastery in Tibet and was built under the direction of Padmasambhava in 740-760 C.E.

31. Up until recently Rechungpa's lineage of instructions were still passed on from one person to another in Sangri. But since the Chinese invaded Tibet in 1959, it is uncertain if this lineage continues. *—Thrangu Rinpoche*

32. The prophecy concerning the hidden terma on sorcery said that in three generations a fortunate being would come and take the terma out. This person was someone who probably was an emanation of Rechungpa. I don't know much about who this was. But it is not a teaching that is practiced very much.
—Thrangu Rinpoche

33. Rechungpa did receive Dawa Drukpa's wife and he gave her teachings and instructions. She then practiced these and became a great meditator. Four years after Rechungpa died, she herself died and when she was cremated there were sacred relics found in her ashes. *—Thrangu Rinpoche*

The Glossary

Amitayus Literally, "limitless life." A meditational deity associated with long life. The long life aspect of Buddha Amitabha.

amrita (Tib. *dut tsi)* A blessed substance which can cause spiritual and physical healing.

Avalokiteshvara (Tib. *Chenrezig*) Deity of compassion. Known as the patron deity of Tibet and his mantra is OM MANI PADMA HUM.

bardo (Tib.) Literally, bardo means "between the two." There are six kinds of bardos, but here it refers to the time between death and rebirth in a new body.

bodhichitta (Tib. *chang chup chi sem*) Literally, the mind of enlightenment. There are two kinds of bodhichitta: absolute bodhichitta, which is completely awakened mind that sees the emptiness of phenomena, and relative bodhichitta which is the aspiration to practice the six paramitas and free all beings from the suffering of samsara.

bodhisattva (Tib. *chang chup sem pa*) An individual who is committed to the Mahayana path of practicing compassion and the six paramitas in order to achieve Buddhahood and free all beings from samsara. More specifically, those with supreme motivation to achieve liberation for the sake of all sentient beings and who are on one of the ten bodhisattva levels that culminates in Buddhahood.

bodhisattva levels (Skt. *bhumi*, Tib. *sa*) The levels or stages a bodhisattva goes through in reaching enlightenment. These consist of ten levels in the sutra tradition and thirteen in the tantra tradition.

bodhisattva vow A vow in which one promises to practice in order to bring all sentient beings to Buddhahood.

Bon or Bonpo (Tib.) The religion of Tibet before Buddhism was introduced. The religion is still practiced in Tibet.

Chakrasamvara (Tib. *khorlo dompa*) A meditational deity which belongs to the annutara tantra set of teachings.

chakravartin (Tib. *khorlo gyurwa*) Literally, he who turns the wheel and also called a universal monarch. This is a king who propagates the dharma and starts a new era.

Chenrezig See Avalokiteshvara.

chod practice (Tib.) This is pronounced "chö" and literally means "to cut off" and refers to a practice that is designed to cut off all ego involvement and defilements. The *mo chod* (female chod) practice was founded by the famous female saint Machig Labdron (1031 to 1129 C.E.).

clear light (Skt. *prabhasvara*, Tib. *ösel*) A subtle state of mind which according to tantric teachings is the state of mind wherein highest realization is attained.

coemergent wisdom (Skt. *sahajajnana*, Tib. *lhen chik kye pay yeshe*) The advanced realization of the inseparability of samsara and nirvana and how these arise simultaneously.

dakini (Tib. *khandroma*) A yogini who has attained high realizations of the fully enlightened mind. She may be a human being who has achieved such attainments or a non-human manifestation of the enlightened mind of a meditational deity.

dharma (Tib. *chö*) This has two main meanings: Any truth such as the sky is blue and secondly, as used in this text, the teachings of the Buddha (also called Buddha-dharma).

dharma treasure See terma

dharma treasurer See terton

dharmakaya (Tib. *chö ku*) One of the three bodies of Buddhahood. It is enlightenment itself, wisdom beyond reference point. See kayas, three.

dharmata (Tib. *chö nyi*) Dharmata is often translated as "suchness" or "the true nature of things" or "things as they are." It is phenomena as seen by a completely enlightened being without any distortion or obscuration so one can say it is "ultimate reality."

disturbing emotion (Skt. *klesha*, Tib. *nyön mong*) The emotional obscurations (in contrast to intellectual obscurations) which are also translated as "afflictions" or "poisons." The three main disturbing emotions are passion or attachment, aggression or anger, and ignorance or delusion. The five disturbing emotions are the three above plus pride and jealousy.

doha See spiritual song.

Dusum Khyenpa (1110-1193 C.E.) The first Karmapa. He was a student of Gampopa and founder of the Karma Kagyu lineage.

Dzogchen (Skt. *mahasandhi*) This is known also as the "great perfection" or atiyoga. It is the highest of the nine yanas according to the Nyingma tradition.

eight worldly dharmas (Tib. *jik ten chö gye*) These attitudes keep one from the path; they are attachment to gain, to pleasure, to praise, to fame, and an aversion or avoidance to loss, to pain, to blame, and having one's reputation lessened.

empowerment (Skt. *abhisheka,* Tib. *wang*) To do a Varjayana practice one must receive the empowerment from a qualified lama. One should also receive the practice instructions (Tib. *tri*) and the textual reading (Tib. *lung*).

fire puja (Tib. *jin sek*) A tantric ritual in which many different substances are burned. There are four different kinds of burnt offerings corresponding to the activities of pacifying, enriching, subjugating, and destroying. Usually this is done at the end of a long practice.

Gampopa (1079-1153 C.E.) Gampopa and Rechungpa were Milarepa's main students. Gampopa established the monastic foundation of the Kagyu lineage. He is also known for writing the *Jewel Ornament of Liberation*.

ganachakra (Tib. *tog kyi kor lo*) This is a ritual feast offering to the protectors and yidams which is usually done at the end of deity practice.

garuda (Tib. *khyung*) A mythical bird which hatches fully grown.

Guhyasamaja tantra (Tib. *sang pa dus pa*) This is the "father tantra" of the anuttara yoga which is the highest of the four tantras. Guhyasamaja is the central deity of the vajra family.

Hevajra tantra (Tib. *kye dorje*) This is the "mother tantra" of the anuttara yoga which is the highest of the four yogas.

illusory body (Tib. *gyu lu*) One of the Six Yogas of Naropa. See the Six Yogas of Naropa.

Kadampa (Tib.) One of the major schools in Tibet that was founded by Atisha (993-1054 C.E.).

Kagyu (Tib.) One of the four major schools of Buddhism in Tibet. It was founded by Marpa. The other three are the Nyingma, the Sakya, and the Gelugpa.

karma (Tib. *lay*) Literally "action." Karma is a universal law that when one does a wholesome action one's circumstances will improve and when one does an unwholesome action negative results will inevitably occur from the act.

kayas, three (Tib. *ku sum*) There are three bodies of the Buddha: the nirmanakaya, sambhogakaya and dharmakaya. The dharmakaya, also called the "truth body," is the complete enlightenment or the complete wisdom of the Buddha which is unoriginated wisdom beyond form and manifests in the sambhogakaya and the nirmanakaya. The sambhogakaya, also called the "enjoyment body," manifests only to bodhisattvas. The nirmanakaya, also called the "emanation body," manifests in the world and in this context, for example, manifested as the Shakyamuni Buddha.

khenpo (Tib.) A title of someone who has completed many years of intense study of Buddhism. It can also mean an abbot of a monastery.

kyang (Tib.) A wild Tibetan ass.

klesha See disturbing emotions.

lotsawa This is Tibetan for "translator."

lung (Tib.) This is a Tibetan word for ritual reading. In order to perform a Varjayana practice, one must have a holder of the lineage read the text straight through (Tib. *lung)*, give an explanation of the practice (Tib. *tri*) and give the empowerment for the practice (Tib. *wang*).

Machig Labdron (1031-1129 C.E.) The most famous Tibetan female saint who established one of the eight main practice lineages. This is the chod practice which literally means "to cut off" and refers to a practice that is designed to cut ego involvement and the resulting defilements. This is the only lineage that was established in Tibet and then went to India.

Mahamudra (Tib. *cha ja chen po)* Literally means "great seal." All phenomena are sealed by the primordial perfect true nature. The Indian siddha Saraha (10th century) is considered the first human master of this meditation lineage and is practiced predominately within the Kagyu school.

mahasiddha (Tib. *drup thop chen po)* A practitioner who has a great deal of realization.

mahayana (Tib. *tek pa chen po*) Literally, the "great vehicle." These are the teachings of the second turning of the wheel of dharma, which emphasize emptiness, compassion, and bodhichitta.

Maitripa (1012-1097 C.E.) A great Indian master who was one of the teachers of Marpa the Translator. He taught Marpa the path of liberation through Mahamudra practice.

mandala offering One of the four ngondro practices. See ngondro.

Manjushri (Tib. *jampalyang*) A meditational deity representing discriminative awareness (*prajna*). Usually depicted as holding a sword in the right hand and scripture in the left.

Marpa (1012-1097 C.E.) A Tibetan translator who made three trips to India and brought back and translated many tantric texts including the Six Yogas of Naropa, the Guhyasamaja, and the Chakrasamvara practices. His teacher was Naropa and he helped establish the Kagyu lineage in Tibet.

Milarepa (1040-1123 C.E.) Milarepa was a student of Marpa who attained enlightenment in one lifetime. His student Rechungpa is the subject of this book.

naga (Tib. *lu*) A water spirit which may take the form of a serpent. It is often the custodian of underground treasures such as texts or actual material treasures.

Naropa (956-1040 C.E.) An Indian master who is best known for transmitting many Varjayana teachings to Marpa who took these back to Tibet. These teachings were destroyed by the Moslem invasion of India.

ngondro (Tib. and pronounced "nundro") Tibetan for preliminary practice. One usually begins the Varjayana path by doing the four preliminary practices which involve 100,000 refuge prayers and prostrations, 100,000 Vajrasattva mantras, 100,000 mandala offerings, and 100,000 guru yoga practices.

nirvana (Tib. *nyangde)* Literally, "extinguished." Individuals live in samsara and with spiritual practice can attain a state of enlightenment in which all false ideas and conflicting emotions have been extinguished. This is called nirvana.

one-taste practice (Tib. *rolpa*) A practice which started with the Buddha in which the monks would beg for food and they would accept everything given in humility. Later in Tibet one-taste referred to accepting all sensory input whether pleasant or unpleasant as the same.

Padmasambhava (Tib. *Guru Rinpoche*) He was invited to Tibet in the ninth century C.E. and is known for pacifying the nonBuddhist forces and founding the Nyingma lineage.

pandita (Tib. *khenpo)* A great scholar.

paramitas, six See perfections, six.

parinirvana When the Buddha died, he did not die an ordinary death that is usually followed by rebirth. His death is the parinirvana because it ended all rebirths since he had achieved complete enlightenment.

path of skillful means The various methods used by buddhas and bodhisattvas to help sentient beings reach enlightenment which takes the pupil's capabilities and propensities into account.

perfections, six (Skt. *paramita*, Tib. *parol tu chinpa*) Sanskrit for "perfections" and the Tibetan means "gone to the other side." These are the six practices of the mahayana path: Transcendent generosity, transcendent discipline, transcendent patience, transcendent exertion, transcendent meditation (Skt. *dhyana*), and transcendent knowledge (Skt. *prajna*). The ten paramitas are these plus aspirational prayer, skillful means, power, and primordial wisdom (yeshe).

phowa (Tib.) An advanced tantric practice concerned with the ejection of consciousness at death to direct where rebirth will take place.

prajna (Tib. *sherab*) In Sanskrit it means "perfect knowledge" and can mean wisdom, understanding, or discrimination. Usually it means the wisdom of seeing things from a non-dualistic point of view.

rolong (Tib.) A Tibetan zombie.

sacred relics (Tib.) Small spherical stones the size of grains of rice that appear usually after the cremation of a realized being. They are considered a blessing of their sacred activity.

sadhana (Tib. *drup tap*) A tantric ritual text which details how to attain meditative realization of a specific deity.

samadhi (Tib. *tin ne zin*) Also called meditative absorption or one-pointed meditation, this is the highest form of meditation.

samaya (Tib. *dam sig*) The vows or commitments made in the Varjayana which can be to a teacher or to a practice.

sambhogakaya (Tib. *long ku*) There are three bodies or realms of the Buddha and the sambhogakaya, also called the "enjoyment body," is a pure realm of the dharmakaya which only manifests to bodhisattvas. See the three kayas.

samsara (Tib. *kor wa*) Conditioned existence of ordinary life in which suffering occurs because one still possesses attachment, aggression, and ignorance. It is contrasted to nirvana.

Samye monastery The first monastery built in Tibet probably in 750-770 C.E.

Saraha One of the eighty-four mahasiddhas of India who was known for his spiritual songs about Mahamudra.

shastra (Tib. *tan chö*) The Buddhist teachings are divided into the words of the Buddha (the sutras) and the commentaries by others on the Buddha's words (the shastras).

shravaka (Tib. *nyen thö*) Literally "those who hear" meaning disciples. A type of realized hinayana practitioner (arhat) who has achieved the realization of the nonexistence of personal self.

siddha (Tib. *drup top)* An accomplished Buddhist practitioner.

siddhi (Tib. *ngodrup*) Spiritual accomplishments of accomplished practitioners.

six realms of samsara (Tib. *rikdruk*) These are the possible types of rebirths for beings in samsara and are: the god realm in which gods possess the disturbing emotion of pride, the asura realm in which the jealous gods try to maintain what they have, the human realm which is considered advantageous because one has the possibility of achieving enlightenment, the animal realm characterized by stupidity, the hungry ghost realm characterized by great craving, and the hell realm characterized by anger.

Six Yogas of Naropa (Tib. *naro chödruk*) These six special yogic practices were transmitted from Naropa to Marpa and consist of the subtle heat practice, the illusory body practice, the dream yoga practice, the luminosity practice, the ejection of consciousness practice, and the bardo practice. These are practiced often in the three-year retreat.

spiritual biography (Tib. *namtar*) These biographies sometimes called hagiographies are special biographies in that they relate to the conduct and spiritual practices that bring the practitioner to realization.

spiritual song (Skt. *doha*, Tib. *gur*) A song of realization spontaneously composed by a Varjayana practitioner. It usually has nine syllables per line.

stupa (Tib. *chö ten*) A dome shaped monument to the Buddha which often contains relics and remains of the Buddha or great bodhisattvas.

subtle channels (Skt. *nadi*, Tib. *tsa*) These refer to the subtle channels which are not anatomical but ones in which psychic energies or "winds" (Skt. *prana,* Tib. *lung*) travel.

sutra (Tib. *do*) These are the hinayana and mahayana texts which are the words of the Buddha. These are often contrasted with the tantras which are the Buddha's Varjayana teachings and the shastras which are the commentaries on the words of the Buddha.

tantra (Tib. *gyu)* Has two basic meanings. First it is Vajrayana practices, in contrast to the sutra path. Second it is the actual texts of the Varjayana practices. There are four classes of tantra texts: the kriya-tantra, the carya-tantra, yoga-tantra, and the anuttarayoga-tantra.

terma (Tib.) Literally, hidden treasure. Works which were hidden by great bodhisattvas and later rediscovered. They might be actual physical texts or sometimes they are hidden in the mind streams of individuals to be revealed at a later date.

ten negative actions (Tib. *mi dge ba chu*) These actions are murder, theft, sexual misconduct, lying, slander, irresponsible chatter, verbal abuse, envy, vindictiveness, and holding wrong views.

terton (Tib.) A master in the Tibetan tradition who discovers treasures (*terma*) which are teachings concealed by great masters of the past.

thangka (Tib.) A Tibetan religious painting.

Tilopa (928-1009 C.E.) One of the 84 mahasiddhas who became the guru of Naropa. These teachings came down from Naropa through the Kagyu lineage.

Trisong Deutsen (790-858 C.E.) Was king of Tibet and invited Padmasambhava to Tibet. He also directed construction of Tibet's first monastery, Samye Ling.

tsampa (Tib.) Roasted barley flour that is a staple of Tibet.

tsa tsa (Tib.) A small clay icon.

Tsangpa Gyare (1162-1211C.E.) The First Drukchen, who is head of Drugpa Kagyu lineage.

tulku (Tib., Skt. *nirmanakaya*) A manifestation of a realized being that is perceived as an ordinary person. The term has commonly been used for a discovered rebirth of a former teacher.

tummo (Tib.) An advanced Varjayana practice for combining bliss and emptiness which produces inner body heat as a by-product.

upasaka (Tib. *genyan*) A lay individual who has taken the five vows of not to kill, not to lie, not to steal, not to take intoxicants, not to engage in sexual misconduct.

upaya (Tib. *tap*) Literally, skillful means. This is used by enlightened beings to present the dharma taking the student's capabilities and propensities into account.

vajra (Tib. *dorje*) Usually translated "diamond like." This may be an implement held in the hand during certain Varjayana ceremonies, or it can refer to a quality which is so pure and so enduring that it is like a diamond.

Vajradhara (Tib. *Dorje Chang*) The name of the sambhogakaya Buddha. The teachings of the Kagyu lineage were transmitted from Vajradhara.

Vajrapani (Tib. *Channa Dorje*) A major bodhisattva said to be lord of power and a major protector of Tibetan Buddhism.

Vajrasattva (Tib. *Dorje Sempa*) The Buddha of purification. Vajrasattva practice is part of the four preliminary practices.

Vajravarahi (Tib. *Dorje Phagmo*) The dakini consort of Chakra-samvara. She is the main yidam of the Kagyu lineage and is the embodiment of wisdom.

Vajrayogini (Tib. *Dorje Palmo*) A semiwrathful yidam of the anut-tara-yoga-trantra. This deity is popular in the Kagyu, Sakya, and Gelug traditions and is usually depicted as red in color.

Varjayana (Tib. *dorje tekpa*) There are three major traditions of Buddhism: Hinayana, Mahayana, Vajrayana. The Vajrayana is based on the tantras and is mainly practiced in Tibet.

vayu (Tib. *lung*) In Sanskrit and Tibetan can mean the "wind" outside or the air that is breathed as well as the subtle airs of the body. Different kinds of vayus regulate different functions; the subtle air that maintains life is called prana. In this context it refers to the subtle airs or energies that travel along the subtle channels.

yidam (Tib.) A tantric deity that embodies qualities of Buddhahood and is supplicated and visualized in the Varjayana. Also called a tutelary deity.

yogi (Tib. *naljorpa*) A Buddhist practitioner who has chosen an unconventional path of practicing.

Glossary of Tibetan Terms

Pronounced	Tibetan Transliteration	English
bardo	bar do	bardo
bon	bon	Bon religion
cha ja chen po	phyag rgya chen po	Mahamudra
channa dorje	phyag na rdo rje	Vajrapani
chang chup chi sem	byamg chub kyi sems	bodhichitta
chang chup sem pa	byang chub sems pa	bodhisattva
Chenrezig	spyan ras gzigs	Avalokiteshvara
chin kor	dkyil 'khor	mandala
chö ten	mchod rten	stupa
chod	chod	chod practice
chö	chos	dharma
cho ku	chos sku	dharmakaya
chö nyi	chos nyid	dharmata
dam sig	dam tshig	samaya
do	mdo	sutra
drup tap	sgrub thabs	sadhana
genyan	dge bsnyen	layman's vows
gyu	rgyud	tantra
dorje	rdo rje	vajra
Dorje Chang	rdo rje 'chang	Vajradhara
Dorje Palmo	rdo rje rnal 'byor ma	Vajrayogini
Dorje Phagmo	rdo rje phag mo	Vajravarahi
Dorje Sempa	rdo rje sems dpa'	Vajrasattva
dorje tek pa	rdo rje theg pa	Varjayana
dut tsi	bdud rtsi	amrita
Dzogchen	rdzogs pa chen po	Dzogchen
gru to	grub thob	siddha
gu tab	sgrub thabs	sadhana
gur	mgur	spiritual song
gyu	rgyud	tantra
gyu lu	sgyu lus	illusorary body
Jampalyang	'jam dpal bdyangs	Manjushri
jik ten cho gye	'jig rten chos brgyad	8 worldly dharmas

jin sek	sbyin sreg	burnt offering
Kadampa	bka' gdams pa	Kadampa school
Kagyu	bka' brgyud	Kagyu school
kang gyok	rkang mgyogs	swift feet
khandroma	mkha' gro ma	dakini
khenpo	mkhas po	pandita
khyung	khyung	garuda
kor lo gyur pa	'khor los bsgyur ba	chakravatin
kor wa	'khor ba	samara
ku	sku	kaya
kuntusangpo	kun tu bzang po	Samantabhadra
kye dorje	kye rdo rje	Hevajra
lay	las	karma
lung	lung	textual transmission
lung	rlun	prana
Machig Drupay Gyalmo	ma gcig 'grub pa'i rgyal mo	Drupay Gyalmo
namtar	rnam thar	spiritual biography
nyön mong	nyon mongs	disturbing emotion
na drup	dngas grub	siddhis
ngondro	ngon dro	prelimin. practices
nyangde	mya ngan las 'das pa	nirvana
nyon thö	nyan thos	shravaka
Phagna Dorje	phyag na rdo rje	Vajrapani
phowa	'pho ba	ejection of consc.
rinpoche	rin po che	"precious jewel"
sang pa dus pa	gsang ba 'dus pa	Guhyasamaja
sherab	shes rab	prajna
tan chö	bstan bcos	commentary
tek pa chen po	theg pachen po	mahayana
terma	gter ma	hidden texts
tap	thab	upaya
thangka	thang ka	spiritual painting
ting ne zin	ting nge 'dzin	samadhi
to pa	thod pa	skull cup
tog kyi kor lo	tshogs kyi 'khor lo	ganachakra
tri	'khrid	dharma explanation
tsampa	rtsam pa	barley flour
tummo	gtum mo	tummo practice
wang	dbang	empowerment
yidam	yi dam	personal deity

Bibliography

The Life of Liberation of the Venerable Rechung Dorje Drak (Tib. *je bhun ras chung rdo rje grags pa'i nam thar rnam mkhyen thar lam gsal ba'i me long ye shes snag ba bzhugs go)*. The work was written by Gotsang Repa who was a pupil of Tsongnyon who is the famous author of *The Life of Milarepa*. These teachings are based on this book and it has not been translated into English.

Chang, Garma (tr.) *The Hundred Thousand Songs of Milarepa*. Secaucus, New Jersey: University Books, 1962. This book gives more detail to Milarepa's life. It contains a large number of spiritual songs of Milarepa, but the translation often leaves portions of the original text out.

Gampopa. *The Jewel Ornament of Liberation* (Tib. *thar pa rgyan*) There is an excellent translation of this work by Khenpo Konchog Gyaltsen Rinpoche in his *The Jewel Ornament of Liberation*. Ithaca, New York: Snow Lion Publications, 1998.

Lhalungpa, Lobsang. (Tr.) *The Life of Milarepa*. London: Granada Publishing, 1979. An excellent translation of the story of Tibet's greatest saint.

Mackenzie, Vicki. *Cave in the Snow: Tenzim Palmo's Quest for Enlightenment.* New York: Bloomsbury Publishing.

Nalanda Translation Committee. *The Life of Marpa, the Translator*. Boston: Shambhala, 1986. A translation of the spiritual biography of Marpa.

Thrangu Rinpoche. *Ten Teachings from the 100,000 Songs of Milarepa*. Boulder: Namo Buddha Publishing, 1999. In this book Thrangu Rinpoche takes ten of the important spiritual songs and describes the events and the practices involved.

The Index